BUILD A TEMPLE TO GOD!

A Retreat with
The Mystical Temple of God
by St. Stanislaus Papczyński

Fr. Paweł Naumowicz, MIC

Copyright © 2024 Marian Fathers of the Immaculate Conception
of the B.V.M. All rights reserved.

Marian Press English language edition published by arrangement
with the Religious House of the Congregation of the Marian Fathers
of the Immaculate Conception of the Most Blessed Mary
in Marianki, Gora Kalwaria, Poland.
First published as *Zbuduj Bogu świątynię!* by PROMIC in 2023.

English translation: *Irena Bartczak*
Copy Editor: *Rachel Salvetti*
Illustrations: *Marek Mikulski*
Composition of the book: *Kathy Szpak*

Available from:
Marian Helpers Center
Stockbridge, MA 01263

Prayerline: 1-800-804-3823
Orderline: 1-800-462-7426

Websites:
Marian.org
TheDivineMercy.org
ShopMercy.org

Library of Congress Control Number: 2024931361
ISBN: 978-1-59614-613-6

Imprimi Potest:
Very Rev. Chris Alar, MIC
Provincial Superior, Blessed Virgin Mary, Mother of Mercy Province
Marian Fathers of the Immaculate Conception of the B.V.M.
February 2, 2024
Feast of the Presentation of the Lord

Nihil Obstat:
Father Thaddaeus Lancton, MIC, STD
Censor Deputatus
February 2, 2024

Note: The *Nihil Obstat* and corresponding *Imprimi Potest* are not a
certification that those granting it agree with the contents, opinions, or
statements expressed in the work. Instead, they merely confirm that the
work contains nothing contrary to faith and morals.

All the biblical passages, unless otherwise stated,
from The New Jerusalem Bible (NJB),
Darton, Longman and Todd and Les Editions du Cerf, 1985.

Table of Contents

Introduction 5
Saint Stanislaus Papczyński 7
CHAPTER 1: To Be Holy and Faultless 13
CHAPTER 2: You are the Temple of God 25
CHAPTER 3: Consecrated Through Baptism 35
CHAPTER 4: Continuous Sacrifice 43
    The Heart as an Altar 43
    Love as a Priest 45
    Sacrifice (*Sacrificium* and *Victima*) 47
    Mortification 51
CHAPTER 5: Around An Altar 57
    Incense of Prayer 60
    The Lamp of the Commandments 61
    The Lampstand of the Seven Gifts of the Holy Spirit ... 63
CHAPTER 6: The Sensory Ministers of the Temple 66
    The Doors of Eyes 72
    The Windows of Ears 73
    Touch 75
    Taste 75
    Smell 77
CHAPTER 7: Take Care of Your Temple 83
    Conscience as a Preacher 83
    The Music of Emotions 85
    Actions as a Roof 87
    Fame as a Bell 89
    Virtues as Ornaments 91

CHAPTER 8: Cleaning and Reconciliation 97
   Restoring the Original Holiness 103
CHAPTER 9: Restoration 113
   Corporal Acts of Mercy 114
   Spiritual Acts of Mercy 118
CHAPTER 10: Eternity 131
   Patron Saints as Guardians 131
   Immortality of the Temple 134
   The Glory of the Temple 136
Conclusion 139
Bibliography 140
About the Author 140
Endnotes 141

Introduction

Most of us have participated, or still participate in various ways, in the construction and maintenance of a temple — a parish church or local or international shrine. But am I aware that God's most important temple, which I should care for, constantly refresh, and beautify, is myself? For each one of us, the question becomes, "What actions do I take to become, through God's power, more Christ-like, more filled with the Holy Spirit, and more radiant with the Divine glory?"

Saint Stanislaus Papczyński, known today as the prophet of the Immaculate Conception, God's champion, and the intercessor of the living and the dead, may serve as a wonderful guide to building and maintaining the temple which you are. Accepting the mystery of the Immaculate Conception of Mary as the center and most important reference point of his life, he founded the Congregation of Marian Fathers of the Immaculate Conception of the Most Blessed Virgin Mary. He wrote a spiritual guidebook, *The Mystical Temple of God* (*Templum Dei Mysticum*),[1] for all people (clergy, laity, and consecrated), so that each of us could draw strength from the mystery of the Immaculate Conception, live that mystery every day, and discover that through Baptism we became a mystical temple of God. He also wrote it in order that every man, by accepting and cooperating with God's grace, could shine ever more brightly with God's holiness in this life and, after death, enjoy the glory of Heaven.

This book has been prepared as an aid for individual retreats made during everyday life. Its basis and main reference is *The Mystical Temple of God*, although the content has been rearranged and modernized. Using *Build a Temple to God!*, you can meditate on whole chapters, parts of chapters, or even smaller fragments of this guide. It is also worth reading St. Stanislaus' original text, which helps us see God's plan for each of us: how we were desired and loved by God before the foundation of the world; became His temple through Baptism;

and are invited to unity with God both here on earth and, ultimately, in eternity.

Let us stand with St. Stanislaus! "[God] chose us ... before the world was made to be holy and faultless before him" (Eph 1:4). Through God's grace of the Immaculate Conception and Mary's cooperation with it, she has been the mystical temple of God from the very beginning and will be so forever. We have become such a temple through Baptism. Walking the path of the Immaculate Conception, under the guidance of St. Stanislaus, we too can become a mystical temple of God forever.

Let's go!

Saint Stanislaus Papczyński

Saint Stanislaus was born on May 18, 1631, in a moderately prosperous peasant family in Podegrodzie, Poland, a few miles from Stary Sącz and Nowy Sącz. He was baptized with the name Jan. Initially, because he had trouble mastering the alphabet, his father removed him from school and assigned him to tend sheep. Through divine intervention, the Saint learned the alphabet in a single afternoon and returned to his studies, first in Podegrodzie and then in Nowy Sącz. At the age of 15, he left his family home and travelled first to Jarosław and then Lviv to further his education.

In Lviv, St. Stanislaus became seriously ill, and it appeared that he would die. Homeless during a freezing winter, he slept on a haystack and couldn't make it to church, even for the celebration of Christmas. Fortunately, people did not allow him to die of hunger and cold, and others sheltered and cared for him. Thanks to their intervention, St. Stanislaus briefly returned to his family home. This suffering, later referred to as his "Lviv Cross," helped him place greater trust in God and, in the future, endure much heavier trials with courage.

He continued his education at the Piarist school in Podoliniec and with the Jesuits in Lviv. The students had to leave Podoliniec due to an approaching plague. From Lviv, because of the nearing Cossack and Tatar armies, they were transferred to the Jesuit college in Rawa Mazowiecka.

In those times, wars, epidemics, and famine constantly plagued the inhabitants of Poland. In Rawa Mazowiecka, the future Saint completed a course in rhetoric and two years of philosophy. He reached the highest level of education attainable for a student of peasant origin.

Saint Stanislaus did not accept the marriage proposal previously planned by his family, instead joining the Order of Clerics Regular Poor of the Mother of God of the Pious Schools, commonly known as the Piarists. There he received the name Stanislaus of Jesus and Mary, which he used for the rest of his life. After two years of novitiate (1654–1656), he took simple vows and soon began teaching rhetoric at Piarist colleges in Podoliniec, Rzeszów, and Warsaw. In 1661, he was ordained a priest and quickly gained recognition as an outstanding preacher, rhetoric professor, writer, confessor, and spiritual director. He heard the confessions of notable individuals, including King John III Sobieski and the Apostolic Nuncio Antonio Pignatelli, later to become Pope Innocent XII.

At the same time, a conflict was brewing between the Saint and his superiors due to his desire for evangelical radicalism, poverty, and orthodoxy. Motivated by his love for the Piarists and guided by a vision engraved upon his heart by the Holy Spirit, St. Stanislaus decided to leave his beloved order to establish a new one in honor of the Immaculate Conception.

On December 11, 1670, St. Stanislaus received an indult that permitted him to leave the Piarist order. Immediately after its public announcement, he made his offering to God (*Oblatio*)[2] within the Congregation of Marian Fathers of the Immaculate Conception of the Blessed Virgin Mary, an order not yet in existence but which he intended to establish. Today, we consider this act of offering as the beginning of the Congregation of Marian Fathers, the first male religious order founded by a Pole with papal approval.

At least since leaving the Piarists, St. Stanislaus chose the mystery of the Immaculate Conception as the center of his spiritual life and the religious order he was founding. Although Blessed Pope Pius IX proclaimed it a dogma only in 1854, St. Stanislaus was completely convinced of its truth more than 180 years earlier.

In the years 1671–1673, St. Stanislaus wrote two very important works: *Norma Vitae* (*Rule of Life*)[3] and *Templum Dei Mysticum* (*The Mystical Temple of God*).[4] *Norma Vitae* was intended for the newly emerging religious order established in honor of the Immaculate Conception. The Rule outlined three specific missions of the Marian order: spreading devotion to the Immaculate Conception; assisting the deceased through prayers, alms, and all works of charity; and supporting diocesan priests in pastoral work. *Templum Dei Mysticum* was written as a spiritual handbook for all members of the faithful and demonstrates how to live the spirituality of the Immaculate Conception in everyday life.

The first house of the new religious order was established by St. Stanislaus in 1673 in Puszcza Korabiewska (the Korabiew Forest), known today as Puszcza Mariańska (the Marian Forest). The second, in 1677, was in Nowa Jerozolima (New Jerusalem, now Góra Kalwaria). Here, the Marian Fathers received charge of the church called the "Cenacle" from the bishop, where St. Stanislaus served for 24 years until his death on September 17, 1701.

Already during his lifetime, St. Stanislaus was highly regarded as a spiritual leader, preacher, confessor, and spiritual director. He was known for supporting the living and the deceased and was seen as a patriot, speaker, writer, ascetic, and healer. Ultimately, he was recognized as a holy man of God.

The fame of his sanctity continued to grow after his death. It saw the most significant expansion at the end of the 20th and the beginning of the 21st century. Subsequent miracles, papal decisions, and actions by Vatican dicasteries allowed for his beatification in 2007 in Licheń and canonization in 2016 in Rome. In 2018, Cardinal Kazimierz Nycz established the Shrine of St. Stanislaus Papczyński in the Cenacle church at Góra Kalwaria.

God waited more than 300 years for the beatification of the Founder of the Marian Fathers. His canonization followed in less than 10 years. We perceive this as a sign that the life and message of St. Stanislaus Papczyński are uniquely relevant to modern times. Although the dogma of the Immaculate Conception was proclaimed by the Pope in 1854, most still largely understand it only as a rational concept, a special privilege granted to Mary because of her Son. Saint Stanislaus deeply understood the mystery of the Immaculate Conception and honored it by founding an order under the title of this mystery and living it every day. He often used the exclamation: "May the Virgin Mary's Immaculate Conception be our salvation and our protection!"

Today, many people come to the Shrine of St. Stanislaus in Góra Kalwaria, especially those desiring a new life in Christ; children and young people struggling with their studies; married couples seeking to conceive children; those entangled in various addictions and dependencies; and those tormented by evil spirits and their own sins. Many are inspired by the life and message of St. Stanislaus and have found in him a guide and intercessor.

"May the Virgin Mary's Immaculate Conception be our salvation and our protection!"

St. Stanislaus Papczyński

CHAPTER 1

To Be Holy and Faultless

In the *Catechism of the Catholic Church*, No. 491, we read:

> Through the centuries the Church has become ever more aware that Mary, "full of grace" through God, was redeemed from the moment of her conception. That is what the dogma of the Immaculate Conception confesses, as Pope Pius IX proclaimed in 1854: "The most Blessed Virgin Mary was, from the first moment of her conception, by a singular grace and privilege of almighty God and by virtue of the merits of Jesus Christ, Savior of the human race, preserved immune from all stain of original sin" (Pius IX, *Ineffabilis Deus*: DS 2803).

The dogmatic definition announced by Blessed Pope Pius IX is remarkably brief, but the mystery of the Immaculate Conception of Mary affects all the most important branches of theology. On December 8, 1998, during his Angelus address, Pope St. John Paul II said, "The Dogma of the Immaculate Conception can be described as a miraculous doctrinal synthesis of the Christian faith. In reality, it encompasses the fundamental truths of revelation."

The mystery of the Immaculate Conception is not merely another privilege of Mary or an element of Mariology and Marian devotion. In this mystery of faith, there is a synthesis of every dogma and all spirituality. It is an invitation for us to "be holy and faultless before him in love" (Eph 1:4) as well.[5]

In the mystery of the Immaculate Conception, the Triune God miraculously reveals His love to man. The Almighty, Who in the death and Resurrection of Jesus Christ gave the greatest proof of His love for each of us and all creation, had to first prepare the Mother. Because of her future motherhood, Mary was preserved from the stain of original sin from the moment of her conception, and, from the beginning of her existence, she was filled with the Holy Spirit. This gift was not due to her merits, as she had not acquired any yet; that gift was given out of God's pure love and grace.

Through the death and Resurrection of Christ, we are lifted up and freed from the bondage of sin, while Mary was preserved from all sin. The mystery of the Immaculate Conception was accomplished by the power of the Paschal mystery; that is, by the power of the passion, death, and Resurrection of Christ. Since the very beginning, the Immaculate Mary is, in a special way, the Daughter of God the Father, the Mother of God's Son, and the Bride of the Holy Spirit. Preserved from original sin by prevenient grace, she responded to it perfectly. She is a new creation, redeemed in the Blood of the Savior. She is a foretaste of the ultimate union between man and God. She is a promise of our reign with Christ in Heaven.

When the Angel Gabriel came to announce the will of God to Mary, he confirmed her complete union with the Trinity. He said: "The Holy Spirit will come upon you, and the power of the Most High will cover you with its shadow. And so the child will be holy and will be called Son of God" (Lk 1:35). Mary, attentive to the Word of God, constantly lives according to the plan and calling that God prepared for her before the ages — even before the foundation of the world. Mary conceives and gives birth to Jesus, cares for Him, and later accompanies Him as His Mother and disciple all the way to the Cross. There, she accepts all people as her children and will never cease to care for us until the end of the world. Free from any sin and filled with the Holy Spirit from her conception, Mary brings Christ wherever she appears. At the sound of her greeting, John leaped for joy in Elizabeth's womb, and she was filled with the Holy Spirit. Mary is among the disciples when the Spirit descends upon them from above on the day of Pentecost. She comes with the Holy Spirit to all who seek refuge in her and imitate her.

Mary's extraordinary union with God, which is a union of the creation with the Creator and the human with her Savior, not only has never been interrupted, but through the Assumption will continue forever. As a new person, perfectly liberated from the bondage of sin and completely devoted to God, she is the eternal enemy of Satan and our powerful Advocate. Wherever Mary is, there God is present. Wherever she comes, without any stain of sin, perfectly united with God, Satan loses his power. According to exorcists, Satan cannot bear the name of Mary, and invoking her intercession defeats him. She not only responds to our cries but, just as at the wedding at Cana, presents to her Son our difficulties and problems of which we are not yet aware. Satan has never had anything of his own in her. Mary, obedient to God in all things, drives out Satan, who refused to obey God.

In our daily spiritual battle, we invoke the intercession of her who, in the power of God, conquers Satan and, as the best mother, entrusts us to the Almighty. In response to the lies of the devil, united with the Trinity from her conception, she proclaims to us the Good News about God, Who is love. Satan deceives us, telling us that God does not care about us, that our lives are meaningless, and that, by turning away from God, we will become like gods ourselves. The Immaculate Mary convinces us that our life has its beginning and culmination in God. She points us to the merciful God, Who loved us before the ages, called us into existence, and chose us "to be holy and faultless before him in love" (Eph 1:4). He does not tire of forgiving, but continually desires to fill us with His love and grace.

The devil deceives us with helplessness and despair, persuading us that there is no hope for us anymore and that our sins are unforgivable. The mystery of the Immaculate Conception points to Jesus, Who died, was resurrected for our justification, and continually says, "Come to me, all you who labor and are overburdened, and I will give you rest" (Mt 11:28). In the Sacraments of Baptism and Penance/Reconciliation, Christ washes us in His blood and creates us anew. In Holy Mass, God announces His Word to us and feeds us with the Body and Blood of Christ, the food for eternal life.

In our daily spiritual struggle, we need to contemplate the mystery of Mary's Immaculate Conception and her whole life and imitate her in every possible way. The Immaculate

Conception invites us to constantly invoke the graces of God the Father, Son, and Holy Spirit, to unite with Him, abide in Him, and worship Him with our thoughts, words, and deeds. Following the example of Mary, we are to constantly praise God for the great things He continually does for us. We are to live by the commandment of love, listen to the Word of God, and remain in the community of the Church. The Immaculate One leads us to the Sacraments that we may be filled with the grace of God through them, rise from sin, and not sin again. Mary shows us that union with God also means finding God and serving Him in others.

Whenever we invoke the intercession of the Immaculate Mary, she always submits us to the Mercy of God, brings us the Holy Spirit, and, pointing to Jesus, repeats, "Do whatever he tells you" (Jn 2:5). She brings us to the place of God's grace, which is always greater than our sin and Satan's wiles. She always leads us to God, the source of all life, that by entrusting our entire lives to Him, we may praise Him together with Mary and the saints, now and in eternity. Mary, Immaculately Conceived, "full of grace," and "all Holy," shows us that only by constantly being united with God and filled with His grace will we have the strength to resist all the actions of the evil one and fulfill the calling that God has entrusted to us, which is that we may be holy as God is holy. "[B]e holy and faultless before him in love" (Eph 1:4).

The mystery of the Immaculate Conception was the central theme of the life and spirituality of St. Stanislaus Papczyński. He did not write a theological treatise on this topic, as there were already enough of them. For St. Stanislaus, the Immaculate Conception was "crystal clear." Therefore, he did not attempt to prove it intellectually. Rather, he decided to live it and promote it.

To spread devotion to the Immaculate Conception, St. Stanislaus founded the Congregation of Marian Fathers of the Immaculate Conception of the Most Blessed Virgin Mary and composed the *Rule of Life*[6] for his confrères. Today, the beginning of the congregation is considered to be the act of self-offering (*Oblatio*)[7] he made on December 11, 1670. In the four main sentences of the act, the Immaculate Conception appears three times. The Marians were to profess this mystery through the very name of the congregation. They were prescribed a white habit "in honor of the Immaculate Conception of Our Lady."⁸ Spreading devotion to this mystery was the first of three specific missions of the new order. The members recited the Little Office of the Immaculate Conception every day. Additionally, they were to establish the Confraternity of the Immaculate Conception of the Blessed Virgin Mary at each of their monasteries. All this began more than 180 years before the proclamation of the Immaculate Conception as a dogma by Pope (now Blessed) Pius IX.

Saint Stanislaus wanted the Immaculate Conception to become a life inspiration, not only for the new members of his order but all people. Therefore, he wrote a handbook of the spiritual life, "for people of every state," entitled *The Mystical Temple of God* (*Templum Dei Mysticum*). The first edition was published in 1675.

In reading *The Mystical Temple of God*, we will seek answers to questions such as, How do we understand the Immaculate Conception? How do we live it out daily? What does it mean for me? What is it, and what can it be in me? What can the spirituality of the Immaculate Conception look like in my life?

Saint Stanislaus assures us that if "anyone reads [his text] with real attention and frequently considers it carefully, he will reap great benefit, namely an increased knowledge of himself and of God, a sure way to salvation and model of Christian perfection."⁹

In the following chapters, we will try to "chew over"¹⁰ the words of St. Stanislaus Papczyński recorded in *The Mystical Temple of God*. However, for now, we will start by meditating on a passage from the Letter of St. Paul to the Ephesians often invoked in the Liturgy of the Hours, which provides a good introduction to reflection on the mystery of the Immaculate Conception and how to live it in everyday life. From the hustle of our work and tasks, God immediately takes us to deep waters to remind us of His love and our election and calling.*

---

* In this and all following quotations, **boldface** emphasis is added by the author unless otherwise noted.

Blessed be God the Father of our Lord Jesus Christ, who has **blessed us with all the spiritual blessings** of heaven **in Christ**. Thus he **chose us in Christ before the world was made to be holy and faultless before him in love, marking us out for himself beforehand**, to be adopted sons, through Jesus Christ. Such was his purpose and good pleasure, to the praise of the glory of his grace, his free gift to us in the Beloved, **in whom, through his blood, we gain our freedom, the forgiveness of our sins. Such is the richness of the grace which he has showered on us** in all wisdom and insight. He has let us know the mystery of his purpose, according to his good pleasure which he determined beforehand in Christ, for him to act upon when the times had run their course: that he would bring everything together under Christ, as head, everything in the heavens and everything on earth. And it is in **him** that **we** have received our heritage, **marked out beforehand** as we were, under the plan of the One who guides all things as he decides by his own will, chosen **to be, for the praise of his glory**, the people who would **put their hopes in Christ** before he came. Now **you** too, in *him*, have heard the message of the truth and the gospel of your salvation, and **having put your trust in it you have been stamped with the seal of the Holy Spirit** of the Promise, who is the pledge of our inheritance, for the freedom of the people whom God has taken for his own, for the praise of his glory (Eph 1:3-14).

Saint Paul starts his letter by praising God: blessed be God, blessed in His work and all He did for us and all the blessings He bestowed upon us. Saint Paul lists here "spiritual blessings," which are in Christ and which were destined for us from the beginning of the world. These blessings (six of them) are identified in the footnotes of your Bible. All of them were fulfilled in the Immaculate Mary, but they are meant to be fulfilled in each one of us also.

1. **"He chose us in Christ before the world was made to be holy and faultless before him in love"** (Eph 1:4). We are chosen by God Himself in Christ. As Mary was chosen to be holy and blameless before the foundation of the world, we were chosen before the foundation of the world. The whole world was created for us. The history of the world proceeded so that I could be born and fulfill my calling. We have been chosen for holiness and purity. This is our primary vocation: to be holy, that is, in union with God the Father, in the likeness of Christ and through Christ, and filled with the Holy Spirit. All this occurs out of love of God and God's love towards us.

It is worth seeing yourself from this perspective: the whole world was moving towards me, waiting for my birth. God was waiting for me before the world was created. Everything was prepared for me to be born, to be holy, and to be united with God in Heaven forever.

2. **"[He] mark[ed] us out for himself beforehand**, to be adopted sons, through Jesus Christ. Such was his purpose and good pleasure, to the praise of the glory of his grace" (Eph 1:5–6). We become holy through adoption. The Immaculate Mary is the daughter of God the Father and the bride of the Holy Spirit through Christ and His salvific power. "We have not come from impurity," says St. Paul. We are adopted children of God, His beloved children, in Christ, with Christ, through Christ, and in the likeness of Christ. This is the center of our life, our dignity, and our calling. Christ is the source and model of my life. Of course, Mary, other saints, or someone living can be spiritual guides in our lives, but the truest, most important guide and reference point of my life is Christ Himself. We are called to live, love, and relate to God and others following His example. We are destined to be sons in the Son and sons in the likeness of the Son. God chose, created, and saved us without any merit on our part, out of His own kindness and grace, in order that we may praise Him with our whole lives. He bestowed His grace upon us in His Beloved Son, Christ.

3. **"[T]hrough his blood, we gain our freedom, the forgiveness of our sins. Such is the richness of the grace**

which he has showered on us" (Eph 1:7–8). Christ saved each of us through His Blood. Mary is saved by Christ and kept from sin. We were redeemed from original and personal sin while we were still helpless sinners. Redemption and forgiveness of sins are accomplished through the Blood of Christ. Christ is willing to shed His Blood for each of us again. My salvation flows from the Cross. I am washed clean of my sins in the Blood of Christ. His Blood is the food for eternal life; it is my refreshment. The Blood shed out of God's love and grace descends upon us in the form of various gifts, including wisdom and understanding.

4. "**He has let us know the mystery** of his purpose, according to his good pleasure which he determined beforehand in Christ, for him to act upon when the times had run their course: that he would **bring everything together under Christ**, as head, everything in the heavens and everything on earth" (Eph 1:9–10). God revealed the mystery of His love and the salvation of man to make everything anew in Christ. The Immaculate One learned God's will in the Annunciation. The mystery had been hidden from the previous generations but was revealed in Christ to His contemporaries, to us, and to those who will come.

> And now to him who can make you strong in accordance with the gospel that I preach and the proclamation of Jesus Christ, in accordance with that mystery which for endless ages was kept secret but now (as the prophets wrote) is revealed, as the eternal God commanded, to be made known to all the nations, so that they obey in faith: to him, the only wise God, give glory through Jesus Christ for ever and ever. Amen (Rom 16:25–27).

> At that time Jesus exclaimed, "I bless you, Father, Lord of heaven and of earth, for hiding these things from the learned and the clever and revealing them to little children." (Mt 11:25).

Everything is destined to be united with God in Christ: Heaven (angels and saints) and earth (saints and sinners). Often, we have many doubts about whether this is still possible, yet God desires to build this unity and is able to do so. He also wants us all to be involved in uniting earth with Heaven and man with God and the angels and saints.

5. "And it is in **him** that **we** have received our heritage, **marked out beforehand** as we were, under the plan of the One who guides all things as he decides by his own will, chosen to be, **for the praise of his glory**, the people who would **put their hopes in Christ** before he came" (Eph 1:11–12). In Christ, the Chosen People — we ourselves (says St. Paul) — become witnesses of the fulfillment of the messianic expectations. Mary gives birth to the Messiah and becomes His disciple. The Jews who accepted the Messiah and placed their hope in Him will exist for His glory, even though there are still many who have not accepted Christ as the promised Messiah.

6. "Now **you** too, **in him**, have heard the message of the truth and the gospel of your salvation, and **having put your trust in it you have been stamped with the seal of the Holy Spirit** of the Promise, who is the pledge of our inheritance, for the freedom of the people whom God has taken for his own, for the praise of his glory" (Eph 1:13–14). In Christ, not only the Chosen People but also the Gentiles (St. Paul says "you") are called to salvation. Whoever believes is sealed with the Holy Spirit. "Whoever believes and is baptized will be saved; whoever does not believe will be condemned" (Mk 16:16). "[I]f you declare with your mouth that Jesus is Lord, and if you believe with your heart that God raised him from the dead, then you will be saved. It is by believing with the heart that you are justified, and by making the declaration with your lips that you are saved" (Rom 10:9–10).

The Holy Spirit crowns the work: the entire Trinity is revealed in its love and action. The Holy Spirit is also a promise of even greater fullness.

It is worthwhile to repeatedly delve into this passage from Ephesians and meditate upon it. It can be read together with the texts of the Old and New Testament cited in the footnotes or side notes of your Bible. The action of the entire Holy Trinity is revealed here in the human being, in me, for my redemption and sanctification, so that we all may live for the glory of God. It is important to see ourselves as desired, awaited, beloved by God and redeemed by Christ. God desired my existence before the foundation of the world, prepared everything for my coming, and made it happen. He gave me a specific calling. Today, He wants to strengthen me anew, embrace me, and assure me of His closeness and love.

God does not withdraw His love. No matter how far I have strayed, He renews His desire for us to be holy and faultless.

Points for personal prayer:

- Allow yourself to be loved by God, in my "here and now."
- Abiding in His love is not an intellectual task but a calling for my heart: embrace the loving God and entrust yourself to Him.
- Thank God [the Father] for the gift of life and love, for His specific calling; Christ for the gift of salvation and the resulting forgiveness of my sins; the Holy Spirit for the constant guidance and sealing of the gift.
- Converse with the Immaculate Mother of God: ask her how she discovered grace, how she expressed gratitude, and how she cooperated with God's grace.
- How does the Immaculate Conception manifest itself in my life? How do I respond to the grace that God bestows upon me?
- May the love of God and God's choice urge us to do good.

"You, Man, are the invention of the Divine deliberation. The most August Trinity raised you up as a Temple for itself, and the Creator of all things called you into being."

St. Stanislaus Papczyński

CHAPTER 2

You are the Temple of God[11]

"It is so certain that Man, created by God, and consecrated to Him through the Sacrament of Baptism, is **His Mystical Temple**, that it ought not to stand in need of proof."[12]

Thus begins the first chapter of *The Mystical Temple of God*, "The Christian is the Temple of God." To support his words, St. Stanislaus Papczyński immediately references two short statements of St. Paul the Apostle from his letters to the Corinthians. Let us recall here slightly longer excerpts from St. Paul's letters than those quoted by St. Stanislaus:

> **Do you not realize that you are a temple of God with the Spirit of God living in you?** If anybody should destroy the temple of God, God will destroy that person, because God's temple is holy; and you are that temple. (1 Cor 3:16–17).

> **Do you not realize that your body is the temple of the Holy Spirit**, who is in you and whom you received from God? You are not your own property, then; you have been bought at a price. So use your body for the glory of God. (1 Cor 6:19–20).

> How can Christ come to an agreement with Beliar and what sharing can there be between a believer and an unbeliever? The temple of God cannot compromise with false gods, and **that is what we are — the temple of the living God**. We have God's word for it: I shall fix my home among them and live among them; I will be their God and they will be my people. (2 Cor 6:15–16).

Saint Stanislaus assures us that we have been created in the Image and Likeness of God. He refers to two descriptions of the creation of man from the Book of Genesis (Gen 1:26–31;

Gen 2:4–25), and other passages from the Holy Scriptures (*see* Ps 144:3; Ps 119:73; Job 10:8) to make us aware of our extraordinary dignity of being like God Himself. Let us recall here only the excerpts about the creation of man:

> God made wild animals in their own species, and cattle in theirs, and every creature that crawls along the earth in its own species. God saw that it was good. God said, "**Let us make man in our own image, in the likeness of ourselves, and let them be masters** of the fish of the sea, the birds of heaven, the cattle, all the wild animals and all the creatures that creep along the ground." **God created man in the image of himself, in the image of God he created him, male and female he created them**. God blessed them, saying to them, "**Be fruitful, multiply, fill the earth and subdue it**. Be masters of the fish of the sea, the birds of heaven and all the living creatures that move on earth" (Gen 1:25–28).
>
> The LORD God shaped man from the soil of the ground and blew the breath of life into his nostrils, and man became a living being. ... Then, the LORD God made the man fall into a deep sleep. And, while he was asleep, he took one of his ribs and closed the flesh up again forthwith. God fashioned the rib he had taken from the man into a woman, and brought her to the man. And the man said: "This one at last is bone of my bones and flesh of my flesh! She is to be called Woman, because she was taken from Man" (Gen 2:7, 21–23).

According to the above descriptions from Genesis, man, created in the image and likeness of God as male and female, is called to love God and one another, be fruitful, and have dominion over the earth. Man, created by God as male and female, is the crown of creation, having dominion over it according to the principles established by God. The descriptions in Genesis are a treatise on our creation, on the calling of each one of us to love, life, and immortality.

We must constantly return to these texts because various ideas continuously arise that seek to obscure or destroy God's plan. Today, as throughout history, certain ideologies attempt to reject the divine image of creation. Referencing the Golden Rule regarding animal treatment is complete nonsense in light of the creation story. The idea of limiting fertility in order to "not harm Mother Earth" contradicts the truth that God has subjected all creation to humanity. The Earth is for man, not man for the Earth. Contemporary homage paid to the Earth is beginning to resemble paganism and an excessive cult of nature, which goes even to the point of idolizing it. The Holy Scriptures clearly state that God created man as male and female. Attempts to convince people that they are the masters of nature and can freely shape their gender are a clear opposition to the Word of God and an attempt to make man into a god.

Saint Stanislaus emphasizes that, during the creation of material things (sun, moon, sea, land...), plants, and animals, God is mentioned in the singular form. ("God said... and it was so.") Only in the creation of man do we read "Let us make man." He comments that only for man's creation does the Creator of the universe, the entire Trinity, seem to engage in a special reflection, a kind of consultation, because He is about to accomplish "something of the utmost and greatest importance." Hence, St. Stanislaus exclaims, "Behold, man, your dignity!" Previously, he called out to Christians with admiration, saying, "What a glory is yours! What a dignity!"[13]

Referring to the Holy Scriptures, he has no doubt that all creation — stars, planets, stones, diamonds, metals, everything that moves in the air, on the sea, and on the earth — in short, everything — has a nature lower than man's nature, for only man, only the human being, "has been made in the image of God." This statement appears several times in the text, like a refrain in a hymn to the glory of God and man. Saint Stanislaus, drawing inspiration from Gennadius from the 5th century, explains in various ways what it means to "be made in the image of God." For example, as God cares for all creation and all people, so too does man care for certain individuals. Just as God is unlimited and can be present everywhere, so man's thoughts can move quickly in space and time. God is the King and Judge of the universe and has entrusted to man the power to judge and discern good and evil. As God is immortal and creative, man also, albeit in a limited way, manifests these same perfections.

Referring to St. Ambrose and St. Bernard of Clairvaux, St. Stanislaus points out other similarities between God and man. Because of the soul, a person exists, lives, and thinks. God is one nature in three Persons, while the soul has one nature and three faculties (memory, intellect, will), corresponding to the three Divine Persons (Father, Son, Holy Spirit), and so on.

Following the example of St. Bernard, St. Stanislaus encourages us to conform ourselves to God in "our quest for peace, our search for truth, and our love of charity."[14] Following the example of St. Ambrose, St. Stanislaus encourages us to be loving, good, just, patient, gentle, pure, and merciful. He urges us to reflect Christ, the Lord and King of all.

Saint Stanislaus states, "You, Man, are the invention of the Divine deliberation. The most August Trinity raised you up as a Temple for itself, and the Creator of all things called you into being."[15] In his writings we find numerous references to the Holy Trinity and its actions. He perfectly distinguishes the Persons of the Trinity, their attributes, and their specificity. He calls God the Father the Creator, the Son of God the Savior, and the Holy Spirit the Sanctifier *(see* "Inscription of the Mystical Temple" at the end of *The Mystical Temple of God*).

Especially in *Examination of the Heart*,[16] St. Stanislaus refers to Mary as the work, dwelling, and temple of the entire Trinity. Similarly, he speaks about man, stating that the Trinity creates and leads men towards their ultimate goal. He calls man "the House of God," "the dwelling of Christ and of His Eternal Father," "the tabernacle of God," and "the Temple of the Holy Spirit." Saint Stanislaus encourages us to praise the Father, Who created us for His glory; to exalt the Son, Who redeemed us out of love for life; and to praise the Holy Spirit, Who enlightens us with His grace.

Saint Stanislaus performed all his most important acts in the name of the Most Holy Trinity. These include the previously mentioned *Oblatio*, or *Self-Offering*, publicly made to God in December 1670; the first and second testaments; the final blessing of his confrères in the second testament; the profession of solemn vows;[17] and others.

According to St. Stanislaus, the Prophet of the Immaculate Conception, God, Who created us out of pure love and grace, without any merit on our part, consecrates us as His mystical temple through Baptism. He "sanctifies" us, "enlightens us with the light of His grace," "dedicates us to Himself," and "restores in us the original righteousness." Quoting St. Augustine, he tells us that "since we have not deserved to become the Temple of God by any previous merits but by the grace of God, let us labor as hard as we can with His assistance to ensure that our Lord may not find anything in His Temple, that is, in us, that offends the eyes of His Majesty."[18] In these words, the light flowing from the mystery of Mary's Immaculate Conception clearly resound: God's grace always precedes and exceeds our sin, but our cooperation with God's grace is required to bear even more abundant fruit.

This is precisely what happened in the Immaculate One: filled with grace, she continually cooperated with the Holy Trinity and in her earthly life brought forth abundant fruit from the freely given grace of God, fruit which she still continuously bears in Heaven.

Saint Stanislaus continues, "Nor is it sufficient to apprehend the mere presence of God; we must also show in our actions and exterior deeds that we truly bear within us the living and unsullied image of God."[19] We approach God through His grace and our cooperation with it. For this reason, in this context he quotes a significant passage from the writings of St. Ambrose, *De dignitate conditionis humanae*:

> [L]et everyone pay more careful attention to the excellence of his first condition and acknowledge the venerable likeness to the Holy Trinity in himself, and strive, by the nobility of his conduct, the exercise of virtues, and the dignity of merits, to possess the honor of divine likeness; so that when it becomes manifest what he is like, then it appears that he is similar to

Him who wondrously formed him in His likeness in the first Adam, and yet more wondrously reformed [him] in the second.[20]

First, we must recognize our dignity as part of God's creation and our divine calling. Because of this dignity, there are no unwanted individuals, and no one lives by chance. God has desired us from the beginning and brought us to this day. Having recognized our dignity as created and redeemed children of God, we can no longer act like pagans in the world — in other words, like "everyone else." We cannot compromise with the world and sin, as St. Stanislaus, the Saint from the Cenacle, continues, since we know that we are created for Heaven and the joyous contemplation of God together with the angels.

In the first two chapters of *The Mystical Temple of God*, the remarkable erudition of St. Stanislaus is already evident. He frequently quotes the Old and New Testament and references Fathers of the Church, saints, and theologians (such as St. Ambrose, St. Augustine, St. Bernard, Gennadius, St. Gregory of Nyssa, Hugh of St. Victor, and St. Lawrence), citing their writings or teachings. In his rhetoric textbook *Messenger of the Queen of Arts (Prodromus Reginae Artium)*,[21] written when still a member of the Piarist Order, St. Stanislaus often referenced ancient Greek and Latin writers and rhetoricians. In *The Mystical Temple of God*, written at the beginning of the founding of the Marian Fathers, there are fewer references like this. We do not know whether he was familiar with the entire works of the saints that he referenced or relied on collections of quotes. However, there is no doubt that he was able to select various statements to strengthen his arguments and make them more universal. This was a common technique in the 17th century, used to demonstrate that the premises the author held were also taught by the Church Fathers and the saints.

Points for personal prayer:

- To what extent am I certain in believing in my dignity as a child of God, a disciple of Christ, a creation of God, and a mystical temple of God?

- Do I constantly think of myself as worthless, as the last one, as irredeemably broken?
- What does it mean for me to be created in the Image and Likeness of God? What does it mean to be the crown of creation?
- What does it mean to me to be a mystical temple of God?
- What kind of temple am I today? To what extent am I God's temple, the devil's temple, or a temple without distinction?
- To what extent do I manifest God and His goodness through my life and actions?
- How do I cooperate with the grace given to me? What more can I contribute? What grace do I want to ask of God? What kind of sanctification?
- Ask for the ability to experience God's grace and the dignity with which He blesses us.
- Thank God for the constant blessings bestowed upon you and the fact that He has called you to life, to faith, to marriage, to the priesthood, or to the consecrated life, and a specific mission.
- Thank God for your history, family, and the "here and now."
- Thank the Holy Trinity for making you Their temple and creating you in Their Image and Likeness.
- Thank the Holy Trinity for wanting to reveal Themselves to the world through you.
- Compose and proclaim your own *Magnificat*: *My soul magnifies the Lord, and my spirit rejoices in God, my Savior, for the Almighty has done great things for me, and His Name is holy.* ...

"It is so certain that Man, created by God, and consecrated to Him through the Sacrament of Baptism, is His Mystical Temple, that it ought not to stand in need of proof."

St. Stanislaus Papczyński

CHAPTER 3

Consecrated Through Baptism[22]

Before we delve into the texts of St. Stanislaus Papczyński, I invite you to read a passage from the Acts of the Apostles regarding St. Peter's visit to the centurion Cornelius. Chapter 10 of Acts begins with the vision that Cornelius had in Caesarea Maritima. The angel explained to Cornelius that his prayers had been heard and that he should send for Simon, also called Peter, in Jaffa. When the servants sent by the centurion were on their way to Jaffa, around noon, Peter had a vision. He saw a large sheet descending from the sky with all sorts of animals, reptiles, and birds on it, which the Jews considered unclean. He also heard a voice saying, "Kill and eat." When he objected, saying that he had never eaten anything unclean, he heard a heavenly command not to call unclean what God had cleansed. After hearing these words repeated three times, the sheet was taken back up into Heaven. Cornelius' messengers arrived at Peter's house and invited him to return with them to their master. When Peter came to Caesarea, Cornelius was already waiting for him, along with his relatives and friends.

> Then Peter addressed them, "I now really understand," he said, "that God has no favorites, but that anybody of any nationality who fears him and does what is right is acceptable to him. God sent his word to the people of Israel, and it was to them that the good news of peace was brought by Jesus Christ — he is the Lord of all. You know what happened all over Judaea, how Jesus of Nazareth began in Galilee, after John had been preaching baptism. God had anointed him with the Holy Spirit and with power, and because God was with him, Jesus went about doing good and curing all who had fallen into the power of the devil. Now we

are witnesses to everything he did throughout the countryside of Judaea and in Jerusalem itself: and they killed him by hanging him on a tree, yet on the third day God raised him to life and allowed him to be seen, not by the whole people but only by certain witnesses that God had chosen beforehand. Now we are those witnesses — we have eaten and drunk with him after his resurrection from the dead — and he has ordered us to proclaim this to his people and to bear witness that God has appointed him to judge everyone, alive or dead. It is to him that all the prophets bear this witness: that all who believe in Jesus will have their sins forgiven through his name."

While Peter was still speaking the Holy Spirit came down on all the listeners. Jewish believers who had accompanied Peter were all astonished that the gift of the Holy Spirit should be poured out on gentiles too, since they could hear them speaking strange languages and proclaiming the greatness of God. Peter himself then said, **"Could anyone refuse the water of baptism to these people, now they have received the Holy Spirit just as we have?" He then gave orders for them to be baptized in the name of Jesus Christ.** Afterwards they begged him to stay on for some days (Acts 10:34-48).

Peter's visit to Cornelius marks a new chapter in the history of the Christian community. Through the intervention of the Holy Spirit, he becomes open to Gentiles who believe in Christ and welcomes them into the community. In a way, we witness three conversions here: Cornelius, who professes faith and receives baptism; Peter, who enters a Gentile's house to make him a disciple of Christ; and the entire Christian community, which henceforth opens its doors to non-Jews (*see* Acts 11:18). In his vision, Peter is cleansed of his Jewish preconceptions: everything is now clean, because it has been purified by God. Peter understands that the Gospel should be preached to Gentiles as it was to the Jews.

When Peter arrives in Caesarea, Cornelius is waiting for him. He has gathered his family and friends to listen to Peter, goes out to meet Peter, and falls at his feet. It is a profound gesture of humility and openness. Here a Roman commander humbles himself before a Galilean fisherman. After some initial explanations, Cornelius declares that everyone assembled is ready, in the presence of God, to listen to Peter. It is worth asking ourselves:

- How is my readiness to listen to God's Word and to God Himself, Who can speak through the least respected and disregarded?
- When and how do I listen to the Word of God?
- When and how do I listen to other people?
- Do I recognize the messengers of the Lord in my husband or wife, parents and children, colleagues, superiors, and subordinates?
- What difficulties, humiliations, and inconveniences do I endure to listen to God?
- What kind of listening does the Lord God expect? In what way does He want to speak?

Peter delivered the *kerygma* to Cornelius, his family, and friends that Jesus, anointed with the Holy Spirit and power, went about doing good and healing all (not only the Chosen People), because God was with Him. Jesus was crucified for our sins and rose again for our justification. The apostles bear witness to all of this, including eating with Him after the Resurrection. All of this has happened in accordance with the words of the prophets and the Scriptures. Those who believe in Him, in His name, receive forgiveness of sins. This is the Good News of salvation available to every sinner.

Peter emphasizes the facts of Jesus' life: John's Baptism, His healings, miracles, death, and Resurrection. He does not reference the Old Testament, knowing he is addressing Gentiles. During Peter's speech, the listeners are filled with the Holy Spirit, begin speaking in tongues, and praise God. No one can doubt that God desires them to be members of the Church. Also, it is unnecessary for them to adhere to the rigorous laws of Judaism because God has already cleansed and sanctified them. All that was required from the Church was sacramental Baptism.

Faith and Baptism brought Cornelius, his household, and his friends into the Christian community, the circle of the saved. After the Resurrection, Jesus said to His disciples: "Go out to the whole world; proclaim the gospel to all creation. Whoever believes and is baptized will be saved; whoever does not believe will be condemned" (Mk 16:15–16). Each of us needs both Baptism and faith for salvation. Most of us have likely already received Baptism. Faith, however, is something we must continuously seek and deepen throughout our lives.[23]

In the 19th chapter of *The Mystical Temple of God*, St. Stanislaus Papczyński identifies Baptism as the consecration (*consecratio* and *dedicatio*) of the mystical temple of God that we are. "The first [consecration] [*dedicatio*] is the one that the Holy Spirit performed in us by the ministry of a priest through the saving Sacrament of Baptism, when He consecrated us [*consecratio*] to Himself."[24]

It is very important here to distinguish between *consecratio* (consecration) and *dedicatio* (dedication). God performs the *consecratio*: choosing us, setting us apart from the state of sin, sanctifying us, and dedicating us to Himself. In response, man performs the act of *dedicatio*: offering oneself to God, surrendering oneself in sacrifice to the One who has loved us.[25]

Quoting Pope St. Leo the Great, St. Stanislaus emphasizes that, through Baptism, we become a temple of the Holy Spirit. Through sin, we drive out the Holy Spirit and become slaves to the devil. Bearing in mind that the price paid for us is the Blood of Christ, we must turn away from sin and live for the glory of God, because the One Who redeemed us out of mercy will judge us in the light of truth.

Today, Baptism is unanimously understood as the Sacrament most closely related to the Immaculate Conception. As she was preserved from original sin and filled with the Holy Spirit in her Immaculate Conception, through Baptism, we are freed from original sin and filled with the Holy Spirit.

Therefore, St. Stanislaus encourages us to solemnly celebrate the day of our Baptism each year as a "second consecration" (*dedicatio*). We should thank God for our consecration and sanctification, which He has accomplished, and renew our dedication to Him.[26]

On the anniversary of our Baptism, St. Stanislaus advises the faithful to observe it with proper diligence, "that they may purify their soul by confession, may receive Holy Communion, and by whatever possible means and diligence they may show themselves most grateful to God for their holy regeneration."[27]

As an exemplary way of "celebrating one's birthday or rather the mystical consecration of the Mystical Temple,"[28] St. Stanislaus provides the example of the Jesuit Fr. Gaspar Drużbicki (1590–1662), as described by Fr. Daniel Pawłowski, SJ (1628–1673), in the work *Vita P. Gasparis Drużbicki Poloni SI*. It is worth noting that both Jesuits promoted devotion to the Most Sacred Heart of Jesus before the revelations to St. Margaret Mary Alacoque (1647–1690), which took place in Paris from 1673 to 1675.

In the "method" of celebrating the anniversary of one's Baptism that St. Stanislaus quotes, the fundamental aspect is giving thanks to God for one's birth, for childhood and youth, for the transition from an unreasoning (animal) state to a rational one. Saint Stanislaus, along with Fr. Drużbicki, expresses gratitude for the fact that he "was born, Lord, into this world, and indeed born blind, indigent, naked, a sinner."[29] He gives thanks that, due to God's care, he "was brought to the font of Baptism and from this reborn to be a son of grace, made a member of Christ and established as an heir of glory."[30] He also gives thanks for his childhood and youth and for growing and maturing.

From thanksgiving, Fr. Drużbicki and, after him, the Marian Founder, move to declaring that, in fulfilling their being, they want to love, honor, praise, and profess God, acknowledging themselves His subjects. Thus, from the *consecratio* performed by God, we want to shift to *dedicatio* — offering our entire selves to God.

The prayer concludes with an offering: "I abandon, expend, immolate, sacrifice, and offer myself as a holocaust to You now, for that time, with all the first fruits of my actions and feelings that are worthy of You and which are due to You from me, in every possible kind of purity, effort and circumstance."[31]

To conclude chapter 19 of *The Mystical Temple of God*, St. Stanislaus adds his own words: "This is how every Christian should spend his birthday [that is the anniversary of his baptism]; and pass his spiritual feast of consecration not in drinking and luxurious revels, but in this thanksgiving."[32] This is, of course, very important advice regarding all the observances of our anniversaries and celebrations.

Points for personal prayer:

- Thank God for your birth and Baptism. Ask Him to allow you to experience being "a child of grace," "a member of Christ," and "an heir to glory" through Baptism. Do you see yourself in this way today?

- Thank God for your entire life as you go through its various stages. Express gratitude for the consecration God wrought in you through holy Baptism and Confirmation, in the Sacrament of Matrimony, in religious consecration, and priestly consecration. Reflect that all of this is the work of the Lord, without any merit of your own.

- Reflect on your way of celebrating Baptism, birthdays, name days, and all anniversaries. To what extent do you celebrate by acts of thanksgiving to God, and to what extent in acts of worldly or even sinful revelry?

- From God's action, we should move to our response, i.e., to *dedicatio*, the offering of ourselves to God. Therefore, this should be thanksgiving that leads to offering.

"The most outstanding and lovable sacrifice of all will be that in which all that is ours, internally and externally, is offered daily to God with a pure intention in such a way that no part of them falls to the lot of the devil."

St. Stanislaus Papczyński

CHAPTER 4

Continuous Sacrifice[33]

A person created by God becomes His mystical temple through consecration (*consecratio*) and dedication (*dedicatio*) performed in Holy Baptism: the consecration is accomplished by the Holy Spirit and the offering (*dedicatio*) is performed by the two people involved (the priest and the baptized). The second dedication (*dedicatio*) always takes place when we celebrate the anniversary of our Baptism. We thank God for our birth and all the stages of our life: for our adoption and incorporation into the Church through Baptism, for our new birth in grace, for becoming a member of Christ and an heir to glory (as St. Stanislaus Papczyński describes it).

The natural result of celebrating one's baptismal, religious, or priestly consecration; consecration of virginity; or the Sacrament of Marriage is making a self-offering to God, including everything we are and possess. In response to the consecration (*consecratio*) that God, through the Holy Spirit, has wrought in us in Baptism, we offer and dedicate (*dedicatio*) ourselves to God alone.

On the anniversary of our Baptism, this offering takes on a special form, but St. Stanislaus recommends that the priest continually offer the sacrifice on the altar of the mystical temple of God. In this temple, the altar is our heart, and the priest is love. The offering should consist of the merits of our Lord Jesus Christ, the life of Mary and the Holy Ones of the Lord, as well as my entire life and all my actions. The Founder of the Marian Fathers desires us to continually offer to God our *dedicatio* and *oblatio*, already made in a special way in the consecration of Baptism.

THE HEART AS AN ALTAR

"And who would not admit that **the Heart of man**, especially of a devout one, **is the Altar of God the Most High?** For, just as God veiled in the most Holy Eucharist is never absent on the altar of a material temple, so He is never absent in a heart that is devoted to Him."[34] Saint Stanislaus, quoting the Book of Proverbs, "My son, give me your heart" (*see* Prov 23:26), immediately exclaims, "For what purpose? That He may inhabit it, reside therein, and stay, reign and rest therein forever."[35]

He references or directly quotes St. Augustine, St. Bernard, Juan Eusebio Nieremberg, and others to emphasize that nothing is more worthy in a person than the heart. That is why "God is to be placed here as on His altar, so that He may rejoice most fully in His whole possession."[36]

Saint Augustine confessed that the human heart is restless until it rests in God. Saint Stanislaus emphasizes that the human heart can only find complete satisfaction in God Himself. "And so it should seek nothing except God, nor to rest anywhere but in Him, to whom it is morally bound."[37]

One can reflect here regarding where I seek fulfillment and peace. Is it in relationships, possessions, titles, knowledge, sports, or appearances? What satisfies me the most today? What triggers feelings of insatiability, unfulfillment, or even defeat in me today?

Saint Stanislaus reminds us of the call of the Lord Jesus: "You must love the Lord your God with all your heart" (Mt 22:37). That's why he admonishes us to "let Him remain alone on His altar. Nothing earthly, let alone impure, should come to rest on it. ... Nor should we permit anything except God on the altar of our heart. ... [T]he slightest disordered feeling toward a small trifle, [or] toward ourselves, very much impedes this perfect love."[38]

Saint Stanislaus encourages us to make our heart, that is, the altar of the mystical temple of God, dedicated and "consecrated to God alone." At the end of chapter 3 of *The Mystical Temple of God*, he exclaims, "O God! Make it that this be so forever."[39]

Points for personal prayer:

- Request an increased awareness that God wants to dwell in your heart as concretely as He dwells in the Most Holy Sacrament of the Body and Blood of Christ on the altar of our material churches.
- It is worth repeating the cry of St. Stanislaus: "O Christian, how great is your glory, how great is your dignity!"
- Ask yourself, to whom is my heart devoted?
- What do I occupy myself with when I have a moment of free time?
- Who or what is my passion? What gives me the greatest joy?
- What is the place of God in my heart, in my life?
- Ask for knowledge of your heart: and knowledge of disordered feelings or disordered attachments. Ask for liberation from them.
- Pray that your entire heart may be dedicated only and exclusively to God.

LOVE AS A PRIEST

"In this Mystical Temple, Love performs all sacred [duties]: **Love, the Priest**, offers all the victims. This Love is pure, holy, fiery, heavenly; it flows from the fountain of eternal Love."[40]

By quoting various authors, St. Stanislaus emphasizes that love distinguishes the children of God from the children of the devil. Therefore, one can engage in various activities, including those that are neutral or indifferent, and, if they are infused with love, they will bear the appropriate fruit. That is why St. Stanislaus emphasizes the need to cultivate the right intention at many different times such as in the morning and evening, when starting a specific task or occupation, at least once during the day — in short, in relation to all the activities we undertake.

"Therefore, whether you are praying, or reading, or writing, or saying good things, meditating, working, eating, drinking, worthily refreshing your spirit, or whatever you do that is virtuous, devout, holy, useful or praiseworthy, do it all out of the love of God."[41]

Today, we could call this practice living an integrated, rational life, subject to reflection. In his time, St. Stanislaus referred to it as living with intention. Our actions should not be completed in a spirit of "just like that," or "to get it done," or "because you have to," but "out of love for God." The intention behind our words, actions, meetings, conversations, and all else that we undertake should be love for God Himself and for Him revealed in our brothers and sisters.

Importantly, love was meant to be the fundamental principle of Marian life (chapter 2 of the *Norma Vitae* is titled "Love"). "Each of you should keep in mind that the soul of his Institute is love, and to the extent that he withdraws from love, he withdraws from life."[42] "Out of love for God," the Marian Fathers are to adhere to *The Rule of Life*, fulfill everything that is good, avoid all evil, and love their brothers and people outside the Congregation. In love, they are to engage in all exercises and tasks entrusted to them, practice mortification, and endure persecution.[43]

Saint Stanislaus teaches his brothers and all of us what is contrary to love: "And so, he will avoid these contagious diseases very opposed to love: envy, hatred, rancor, rivalry, suspicion, calumny, exclusive attachment, antipathy, jealousy, secret accusation, jeering, whispering, verbal abuse, annoyance, ambition, contempt for others, disturbances, agitations, quarrels, contentions."[44]

Points for personal prayer:

- What are the intentions behind my actions and my life?
- Why do I go or not go to Mass?
- Why am I drawn to some people and avoiding others?

- Are these actions done out of love, convenience, pleasure, or profit?
- Which of my actions are truly motivated by love?
- Which have motivations contrary to love?
- What can I do in this matter?

SACRIFICE (*SACRIFICIUM* AND *VICTIMA*)

Two chapters speak about the offering made in the mystical temple: Chapter 4 deals with *sacrificium*, which is more about the attitude of the offering, intention, and act of offering; and Chapter 6 focuses on *victima*, which refers more to the sacrificial victim and the material used for the offering.

Saint Stanislaus teaches that everyone can offer to God who they are and the life they are currently living. A person in distress can offer his "contrition, the righteous his humility, the Priest his praise, the Religious his vows."[45] Pleasing to God is the offering of the afflicted, especially when they praise their Creator and Redeemer amidst their suffering. Pleasing is repentance from a contrite sinner, as well as the prayer of a humble person. Pleasing to God are the prayers of adoration on the lips of priests and the lives of monks dedicated to God in chastity, poverty, and obedience. We could certainly add here that pleasing to God is the fidelity and love of spouses, family harmony, forgiveness of our persecutors, and so on.

Saint Stanislaus emphasizes that among the offerings mentioned, the most precious and pleasing to God is offering all daily internal and external matters to Him "with a pure intention in such a way that no part of them falls to the lot of the devil."[46]

In this context, it is valuable to recall the offering (*Oblatio*) that St. Stanislaus made to the Lord when beginning the process of founding the Congregation of Marian Fathers of the Immaculate Conception of the Most Blessed Virgin Mary. On December 11, 1670, in Kraków, he read aloud a text prepared for this purpose:

In the name of our Lord Jesus Christ Crucified. Amen.

1. I, Stanislaus of Jesus and Mary Papczyński, ... **offer and consecrate to God the Father Almighty, and to the Son, and to the Holy Spirit, and to the Mother of God the Ever-Virgin Mary conceived without the stain of original sin**: my heart, my soul, intellect, memory, will, emotions, whole mind, whole spirit, interior and exterior senses, and my body, **leaving absolutely nothing for myself**, so that from this moment forward I may be wholly the servant of this same Almighty God and of the Blessed Virgin Mary.

2. Therefore, I promise that I will serve them **chastely** and zealously until the end of my life in this **Society of Marian Fathers of the Immaculate Conception** (which, by God's grace, I intend to found) ... .

3. Moreover, I promise reasonably understood **obedience** to His Holiness, the Vicar of Jesus Christ and to his delegated power, as well as to all my mediate and immediate Superiors, and that **I shall not possess anything** privately, but will consider everything as common property.

4. **I confess that I believe** everything which the holy Roman Church believes and everything that she will henceforth teach to be believed. Particularly, I confess in truth **that Mary, the Most Holy Mother of God, was conceived without the stain of original sin, and I promise that I will promote and defend her honor even at the cost of my life**. So help me God and this holy Gospel of God.[47]

The Founder of the Marian Fathers makes his *Offering* (*Oblatio*) in the name of "Our Lord Jesus Christ Crucified." It is important to note that for St. Stanislaus, the central reference point for his entire life was Christ Crucified. He dedicated two collections of meditations to Him: *Orator Crucifixus* (*The Crucified Orator*)[48] and *Christus Patiens* (*The Suffering Christ*).[49] In 18th-century paintings and prints, he is always depicted holding the Cross of Christ.

He dedicates himself to God in the Trinity and to the "Mother of God the Ever-Virgin Mary conceived without the stain of original sin." Here, three Divine Persons and three titles of Mary are mentioned: the Mother of God, the Virgin, and the Immaculate. The order of these titles is very significant. Everything in Mary happened because of her vocation as the Mother of the Son of God. Because of Him and in His power, she was filled with the Holy Spirit from the moment of her conception (she was without original sin) and remained a Virgin forever.

For St. Stanislaus, the act of *Oblatio* is the complete offering of oneself to God, giving up everything one is and possesses, leaving nothing behind. It is surrendering oneself as a burnt offering, with no exceptions. For St. Stanislaus, *Oblatio* meant the complete offering of himself to God in the Order of Marian Fathers of the Immaculate Conception of the Blessed Virgin Mary, offering himself through religious profession and the three vows.

Let's return to the chapters of *The Mystical Temple of God* regarding the offering. After the introduction, the author presents two possible ways of making a daily (morning and evening) **offering** (*oblatio*), one according to the Carmelite John of Jesus and Mary (1564–1615), another by St. Stanislaus himself. The offering of Christ to the Eternal Father for the atonement of sins, familiar to us from the Divine Mercy Chaplet, is like a tiny part of the offering that St. Stanislaus proposes to us.

He offers to the one God from the very beginning of time the merits of the Lord Jesus Christ, Mary, and all the saints, as well as the good deeds of all people. This is an offering that atones and purifies from sins and imperfections both the one who prays and the entire world. The offering is also made for the reversal of punishments and plagues, the removal of dangers, the love of God above all else, and the love of one's neighbor with "ordered love." It is made for the conversion of sinners, the Church, and the whole world.

For example, people come to the Shrine of St. Stanislaus Papczyński at Marianki in Góra Kalwaria to confess their sins on the First Saturday of the month as an act of reparation to the Immaculate Heart of Mary. Others offer their sacrifices and fasts in atonement for the sins of the world and the conversion of sinners. Some offer specific prayers for priests, while others do so for their families or the deceased.

In the second part of the suggested prayer, St. Stanislaus offers himself entirely to God, in order to love Him more and to serve Him better. He offers his heart to God, so that it loves only Him and all others for His sake. He offers his soul, intellect, memory, will, all external and internal senses (which we also know from *Oblatio*), all faculties and abilities, intentions and deeds, desires and plans, feelings, temptations, joys and sorrows, health and sickness, life and death. He concludes his lengthy enumeration of offering in this way: "namely my entire being, and all I have." He ends with:

> Grant, Lord, that I may be wholly Yours and not my own, for all time, at every moment, for the whole of eternity. May all these things be for Your glory, for the honor of the most Holy Virgin Mary, and all who dwell in Heaven, for my salvation and that of my neighbors, and the increase of virtue, and the growth of grace and merit. Amen.[50]

Saint Stanislaus also recommends making a daily **protestation** to God that we do not want to think, speak, or act against His will. He declares that if it should happen, it would be contrary to his will and intentions. "[A]nd that it may not happen, I most humbly beg Your Majesty having regard only for the love of You and Your glory."[51]

It is very characteristic and, simultaneously, in accordance with the message of the Immaculate Conception, that here he expresses the desire to not only rise from sin but also not to fall into sin at all. He would have nothing from the devil and desires that everything within himself (thoughts, words, deeds) be only from God and for the glory of God. He assures us: "By such offerings and protestations we avoid many evils and achieve much good; most importantly, we are made most pleasing to God."[52] Avoid evil and accumulate good: that is our goal.

Points for personal prayer:

- From gratitude for our consecration (*consecratio*) completed by God, I will move on to offering myself completely to the One God (*dedicatio* and *oblatio*).

- It is worth writing our own offering to God according to our baptismal, virginity, religious or priestly consecration, or the Sacrament of Marriage. Each subsequent consecration and each subsequent Sacrament are only an expansion of our first Baptismal consecration.

- Write an offering and read it before the Lord. Over time, you can modify, complement, and expand on it. It is important to be generous in our offering, to trust God, and not be led by our fears or uncertainties. God can accomplish things in us that we would never achieve on our own.

- The act of offering oneself (*oblatio*) can be added to the offering of the gifts of bread and wine (*oblata*) on the Lord's altar during the upcoming Eucharist.

- Today, I want to make another consecration of my temple to God, another offering of myself to my Creator and Redeemer.

MORTIFICATION

In chapter 6 of *The Mystical Temple*, St. Stanislaus presents as an offering (*victima*) "**mortification, both interior and exterior**, but in such a way that it is sacrificed by the Love, the Priest, and we wish everything else in the Mystical Temple to look entirely to him. For whatever is done without him in the Temple is entirely illegitimate and deceptive."[53]

Father Stanislaus includes mortifications of the will, judgment, and imagination among internal mortifications.

Mortification of the will is achieved through obedience to God, the Word of God, ecclesiastical and religious superiors, confessors, and spiritual fathers, as well as pious individuals. Saint Stanislaus distinguishes between the "divine will inspired by God" and the "written rule of the divine will." The "divine will inspired by God" can be the Holy Spirit, pious individuals, sermons, conversations, and more. Many people have converted or taken up God's mission after hearing a passage from Scripture, a good conversation, or the advice of a spiritually-experienced person. According to St. Stanislaus, the "written rule of the divine will" is conveyed to us through commandments, the Gospel, and Scripture in general, liturgical regulations, rules of religious orders, Church laws, and civil laws, as long as they are not tainted by sin or evil intent.

The highest norm and rule is Christ Himself, His life, and His teaching. Saint Stanislaus rhetorically asks: "If one is not persuaded by the life and teaching of Christ to pursue virtue and holiness, who would persuade him?"[54] Following the norm of Christ and looking at His obedience to the Father, he recommends always following the will of others rather than one's own, as long as that does not lead to sin or error. Today this principle may indeed seem outdated, when the world tells us that everyone should follow their own will, and make their own choices, without being concerned about anyone or anything else. How much better married couples would live if they submitted to each other's will! How much better children would be in practicing obedience to their parents, priests to their bishop, and religious to their superiors!

The mortification of judgment, as St. Stanislaus calls it, refers to yielding in a discussion even when victory is clearly on our side. "It is a conspicuous and rare virtue: to allow oneself to be conquered by another when you have victory at hand. Yet I do not want anyone to be silent, when it is necessary to speak, or give way, when he should prevail, especially if the dangerous opinion, or the less probable teaching, or indeed one that is already rejected, is advanced or defended. ... [M]y intent is not to withdraw from fighting for the truth and defending it."[55]

It's worth examining the discussions we have in our families, religious communities, and workplaces. How often do huge arguments erupt over matters that are ultimately of little significance and certainly not worth waging domestic wars over, such as, was there a foul or not in some sporting match? Did we agree on Tuesday or Wednesday? Are vaccinations good or bad? Who won a particular championship? Is one political party better than another? It is a great art to yield in a discussion, even if objectively we are right. Only when matters are of the utmost importance and the consequences of error can be very detrimental to the participants should we resist.

Saint Stanislaus strongly encourages **mortification and restraint of the imagination**, "when less virtuous images flow into it."[56] He is aware that the imagination is like a spirited horse difficult to control. Sometimes, it is necessary to let the images pass on their own and calm down. However, it is always important to train ourselves to master the imagination, so that, rather than living in subjection to it, ultimately, we direct it. In this context, it is important to provide the imagination with good material through appropriate experiences such as travel, music, literature, art, conversations, meetings, etc.

Saint Stanislaus encourages us not to despise **exterior mortification**, because "it is salutary and very advantageous."[57] It involves making sure that "each of our senses performs its dutiful action": sight, hearing, touch, taste, and smell.[58] There will be more about this in the following chapters. The goal is for the body to become obedient to reason and the spirit.

Accepting all difficulties and adversities for the love of God can also be a perfect "offering pleasing to God." However, reason should always guide mortifications and passions. Reason is like a helmsman or a driver. Without it, passion will sink our ship to the bottom of the sea or lead our cart into the field. The passage about mastering passion, which, according to St. Stanislaus, makes a person wise and holy, is beautiful:

I allow you to grow **angry**, but without sin; to **rejoice**, but in the Lord; to **grieve**, but because sometimes you have offended God, who is the highest good, or your neighbor; to **hope**, but for the Kingdom of Heaven; to be consumed with **sorrow**, but in penitence for evils you have committed or good deeds you have omitted; to fear, but only God, as a son fears his father; to **love**, but this same God alone, or, for His sake, your neighbor, and much more so your enemy.[59]

Saint Stanislaus concludes the entire discourse on mortifications as an offering with a simple call that every offering be made by the Priest, Love.

Points for personal prayer:

- What I offer God every day? How do I offer it?
- What in my life is still outside the influence and power of the Lord?
- What am I trying to keep only for myself?
- What would God like me to abandon and offer to Him?
- What mortifications do I undertake? To which ones does the Lord invite me?
- What mortification can and should I undertake for the love of God and my neighbor?

"Assuredly this Mystical Temple of God may be considered most desolate when the incense of constant prayer is not burnt in it. Oh happy Temple, in which this lamp of the commandments of God is never extinguished! It is necessary that every Christian shine with this sevenfold light of the Holy Spirit if he would like to be considered as a true and natural offspring of Christ."

St. Stanislaus Papczyński

CHAPTER 5

Around An Altar[60]

Before we delve into the movable furnishings of our mystical temple (the censer, lamp, seven-branched candlestick, and decorations), we will begin this chapter by reflecting on the passage from St. Matthew's Gospel that speaks of the prayer of Jesus in the Garden of Gethsemane:

> Then Jesus came with them to a plot of land called Gethsemane; and he said to his disciples, **"Stay here while I go over there to pray."** He took Peter and the two sons of Zebedee with him. And **he began to feel sadness and anguish**. Then he said to them, "My soul is sorrowful to the point of death. **Wait here and stay awake with me."** And going on a little further **he fell on his face** and prayed. **"My Father,"** he said, **"if it is possible, let this cup pass me by**. Nevertheless, let it **be as you, not I, would have it**." He came back to the disciples and **found them sleeping**, and he said to Peter, "So **you had not the strength to stay awake with me for one hour? Stay awake, and pray not to be put to the test**. The spirit is willing enough, but human nature is weak." Again, a second time, he went away and prayed: "My Father," he said, "if this cup cannot pass by, but I must drink it, **your will be done!"** And he came back again and **found them sleeping**, their eyes were so heavy. Leaving them there, **he went away again and prayed for the third time, repeating the same words**. Then he came back to the disciples and said to them, "You can sleep on now and have your rest. Look, the hour has come when the Son of man is to be betrayed into the hands of sinners. **Get up! Let us go!** Look, my betrayer is not far away." (Mt 26:36–46).[61]

Jesus returns to His disciples three times and each time finds them asleep. He experiences loneliness, fear, and trembling and sweats blood. He spends three hours before God to surrender His natural will. He keeps asking: "My Father, if it is possible, let this cup pass me by. Nevertheless, let it be as you, not I, would have it."

Here, Jesus completely veils His power and reveals instead the human fear of suffering and death. He resists suffering but also wants to fulfill the Father's will. Jesus' vigil in the Garden is a struggle to remain faithful to God's call. He shows that to persevere in God's will, long prayer is needed, but not prayer filled with words. The more challenging the situation, the more serious the choices, and the greater the suffering, longer and more persevering prayer is required. Jesus often prayed for an extended period, such as before choosing and calling the apostles: "Now it happened in those days that he went onto the mountain to pray; and he spent the whole night in prayer to God. When day came, he summoned his disciples and picked out twelve of them; he called them 'apostles'" (Lk 6:12–13).

In the Garden, Jesus tells the Father that if He must drink the cup of suffering, He will. If we were to approach this situation from our perspective, we might argue with the Father, trying to convince Him of what is better for the Son, the Father, and the world. Jesus has said His peace and leaves the decision to the Father. Sometimes, we demand explanations from God before agreeing to His will or accepting events that affect us. In our interactions with people, we often say, "Please provide me with reasons" before we agree with the justification and become convinced or enter a situation resulting from decisions of ecclesiastical or secular authorities, parents, spouses, etc.

Jesus does not ask the Father for justification. He asks to be spared suffering but ultimately prays for the fulfillment of the Father's will. It is worth asking God to help us reach a point where we can renounce our arguments and trust in the Father's will. It is worth asking, what does my prayer look like in times of suffering or adversity? Am I asking for the fulfillment of God's will in my life, or am I more focused on the fulfillment of my desires? What do I place beneath the words "thy will be done" in the Lord's Prayer every day? Embracing the invitation to become more Christ-like also means embracing the call to accept God's will in suffering.

In the Garden, at the beginning of His Passion, Jesus asks the chosen disciples, those weak people, for help, to stay awake and pray with Him. When He comes to the disciples after an hour, He is strong enough that their help is no longer necessary. He reproaches Peter for the disciples' weakness: "Could you not watch with me one hour?" Then He calls, "Watch and pray that you may not enter into temptation." Pray, that you do not fall into temptation; do not pray for me. Now pray for yourselves, for endurance and strength. When Jesus returns to the disciples again, He does not even awaken them but allows them to remain in their bliss. After the third return, He calls them to rise and go out to meet the enemy.

After three hours, Jesus returns transformed. He is ready to face the crowd with swords and clubs on His own. During Jesus' prayer, the apostles sleep; they do not understand why Jesus brought them to the Garden in the middle of the night, why they should keep watch as if they could not pray the next day. They feel uncertain and sad and do not know how to cope with these feelings. They either cannot or do not want to pray with Jesus, and, as a result, they may be well-rested but still fearful and unsure.

Here I can ask myself and Jesus, where do I escape in difficult situations? Is it into work, sleep, questionable relationships, excessive TV or internet use, alcohol, pornography, gossip, or constant complaining about the government, the Church, superiors or subordinates, spouse, family, brothers, or sisters? All of these are escapes from my vocation. Jesus doesn't escape; He prays "until the end" before facing these fears and dangers. It is worth examining my prayer, my perseverance, and my submission to God in this context.

Daily prayer is a kind of security. Staying with Christ through daily contemplation of the Word is an entrance into His desire for us to accompany and abide with Him. In his meditation on Mount Tabor on February 24, 2013, Pope Benedict

XVI exhorted his listeners to "first of all, the primacy of prayer, without which the entire commitment to the apostolate and to charity is reduced to activism."

INCENSE OF PRAYER

Saint Stanislaus Papczyński believes that we should continually burn the incense of prayer on the altar of our hearts. "Assuredly this Mystical Temple of God may be considered most desolate when the incense of constant prayer is not burnt in it."[62]

Prayer has a far greater power than any of our other actions. "Such souls as these, steadfast in their zeal for prayer, can help the whole Church more in one moment than all preachers with their sermons, Teachers with their lectures, [and] confessors with the administration of penance. They can rouse the dead to life, recall the wicked to righteousness; they can destroy whole armies, avert famine, chase away disease, and do all things being supported in their prayer by two arms, faith and charity."[63]

The Marian Founder recommends that you choose for yourself "fixed prayers, which you should never discontinue, ... what I would advise for your benefit ... Make it your habit also to recall with devotion the Lord's Passion, the four last things, the life of Jesus Christ, the most holy Virgin and the saints."[64] Permanent prayer can also be meditation on the Word of God, adoration of the Blessed Sacrament, the Liturgy of the Hours, the Rosary, the Chaplet of Divine Mercy, the Stations of the Cross, and many others. It is important to establish your own prayer plan for each day, week, and month. Choose a time, place, and form of prayer and stick to it. Periodically reflect on and evaluate your plan. This way, we can receive guidance on how to follow, love, and imitate Jesus.

Saint Stanislaus assures that for prayer, love of God and humility are sufficient. With these two virtues, "the Holy Spirit will teach you to pray. He will supply you with incense, He will kindle it, He will increase the flames and He Himself will accept the most sweet aroma."[65]

At the beginning of his pontificate, Pope Francis said, "Anyone who does not pray to the Lord prays to the devil."

Prayer is the first home of a Christian and his or her primary task. Saint Paul recommends: "Always be joyful; pray constantly; and for all things give thanks; this is the will of God for you in Christ Jesus" (1 Thess 5:16–18). From prayer, we set out in the morning to our daily tasks and return to it in the evening. Unceasing prayer is constantly entrusting ourselves to God, uniting ourselves with Him, and living according to His Word and will. It includes worship, gratitude, adoration, repentance, and supplication. It encompasses both dedicated time for prayer and continually walking in God's presence and love throughout our day.

Points for personal prayer:

- What does my individual and communal prayer look like?
- How important is prayer in my life?
- What are my designated times for prayer throughout the day, week, and month?
- If I lack time, what do I give up first? Sleep? Rest? Meals? Social gatherings? Prayer? Why?
- How much of my prayer includes listening to God and adoring Him? How much includes speaking to Him? How much is thanksgiving and worship, and how much is asking for myself and others?
- What are my favorite, preferred prayers?
- What can I do to make my prayer an even more life-giving meeting with my Creator and Redeemer, Father and Sanctifier?

THE LAMP OF THE COMMANDMENTS

The lamp standing before the altar of the heart represents the Divine commandments. Saint understands the commandments firstly as the directives found in the Holy Scriptures, guiding us toward eternal life. "For just as we know by which way to go when a torch is borne before us, and do not slip off the beaten tracks, in like manner when the **precepts of God** are fixed in the heart and shine in the soul, we best see how to order our present life, and by conforming it to these, we shall by no means turn aside from the path to the eternity of happiness."[66]

Saint Stanislaus recognizes that the first laws were those of nature and the light of reason. When nature was corrupted by sin, God gave His Law, ultimately expounded and fulfilled in Christ. The Church establishes its own laws, which do not add anything to divine laws but clarify them. Finally, various "political associations" and "whole nations" also create their laws. If these laws are just, St. Stanislaus continues, they should be obeyed.

Saint Stanislaus recommends a Christian always keep God's commandments "in his memory, to consider them with his intellect, and fulfill them in his actions."[67] "In addition," St. Stanislaus adds, "the following should be carefully noted. In observing any laws, the correct order should be kept, thus: the first honor should be given to divine laws, then to ecclesiastical, and finally to civil laws. On this score those Pseudopoliticians ought to consider whether the system of state [*ratio status*] is good, which opposes the law of God or the Church?"[68]

A few years ago, a debate erupted in Poland over whether an obstetrician must tell a woman the hospital where she could undergo a legal abortion. Some ethicists argued that since the doctor works in a state hospital, he or she must comply with the state's directives. Unfortunately, similar explanations were given by the Nazis when they were killing civilians at the beginning of the Warsaw Uprising or implementing plans to exterminate Jews: those were state orders and laws.

Some people also argue that although they are Catholics or Christians, when they enter the legislature, office, workplace, or attend a meeting, they must set aside their faith. They use this to explains actions that contradict God's will. Saint Stanislaus is incredibly clear on this matter: one should always adhere to the hierarchy of laws and values. First come the laws of God, then the Church's laws, then civil laws. Being in harmony with God's will is far more important than gaining the support of voters, receiving a bonus from a superior, applause from subordinates, or likes on Facebook.

Many times in chapter 8 of *The Mystical Temple of God*, St. Stanislaus repeats, "Keep the commandments." He also says, "Oh happy Temple, in which this lamp of the commandments of God is never extinguished! ... kindle within you the eternal fire of the lamp of Divine Law ... As this lamp burns and shines forth in your hands it will lead you to the light of the beatific vision."[69]

Expanding on the teachings of St. Stanislaus with the saying of the Desert Fathers, we could say, keep the commandments, God's laws, and the laws of the Church; maintain order and discipline, and they will preserve you.

Points for personal prayer:

- What is the hierarchy of laws that I obey?
- When do I give up God's law for the sake of convenience, support, or higher income? What can I do about it?
- What does my reading and reflection on the *Catechism of the Catholic Church*, Church documents, papal statements, and legal and liturgical regulations at various levels look like?
- What will I do to better understand God's laws and the laws of the Church?

THE LAMPSTAND OF THE SEVEN GIFTS OF THE HOLY SPIRIT

Saint Stanislaus quotes St. Isidore's statement that the seven-branched lampstand in the Jerusalem temple was "the image of the Holy Spirit, who by His sevenfold grace sheds light on the entire Church standing firmly in the unity of faith."[70] He continues, "Therefore, it is necessary that every Christian shine with this sevenfold light of the Holy Spirit if he would like to be considered as a true and natural offspring of Christ."[71]

He lists and briefly characterizes the seven gifts of the Holy Spirit that we should seek to develop:

- **Wisdom** is to be "divine, not human." This means it should love true and avoid false things, do good selflessly, and endure rather than inflict evil. A wise person does not fabricate things but lives in truth. They do not seek revenge for harm done to them and rejoice when persecuted for the sake of truth and honesty.

- **Knowledge** is "knowing those things that are necessary for salvation."[72] Today, knowledge is a great treasure. Many people spend years acquiring knowledge in various fields. However, here St. Stanislaus refers to knowledge leading to salvation. It is worth asking ourselves, what knowledge do I particularly esteem and seek? In which field would I like to be an expert? Is it politics, sports, technological advancements, or financial investments? To what extent do I want to improve my knowledge leading to salvation?

- **Understanding** means "discernment and orderly use of things."[73] This is discerning good and evil, then choosing the good and rejecting the evil.

- **Counsel** teaches "what is to be done, in what place, at what time, by what means and to what end."[74] It also involves guiding others to choose good and avoid evil, grow in virtues, and strive for Heaven.

- **Fortitude** "has its place in undertaking difficult tasks out of love for God, and with perseverance completing them, in overcoming temptations, in enduring adversities with a joyful spirit."[75] Today, courage is increasingly needed to profess faith at school, home, work, and among family and friends.

- **Piety,** according to St. Stanislaus, is related to the worship given to God and to respect and love towards parents and elders. Piety is the act of giving to God what rightfully belongs to Him, such as worship and gratitude, and, ultimately, one's entire life. Without the help of the Holy Spirit, a person cannot be pious, just as no one "is able to say, 'Jesus is Lord' except in the Holy Spirit" (1 Cor 12:3).

- **Fear of the Lord** "diverts one from evil."[76] In order not to lose His grace and closeness, it allows us to endure many hardships and adversities in life.

It is interesting to note St. Stanislaus' explanation of how each one of the seven gifts of the Holy Spirit was present in the martyrs. Without all these gifts, they would not have been able to accept martyrdom.

There is no doubt that, in his time, the 17th century, our Saint was a special advocate of the role of the Holy Spirit. In *Examination of the Heart*, he mentions and invokes the Holy Spirit many times. Let us quote just two examples, the first from the Sunday within the octave of the Ascension, and the second from the Sunday "*In Albis*," After Holy Communion:

> Consider that the Holy Spirit comes to us for a threefold reason: 1) to set on fire; 2) to console; and 3) to convict. ... [I]mplore that the grace of the Holy Spirit may rest in you always: if you become lukewarm may you be inflamed by this grace ... Consider that if the desire to imitate the life of Christ, and especially His Most Holy Passion, is instilled in your heart, you have certainly obtained in the Most Holy Sacrament of the Eucharist the true Spirit of the Lord. For this is an infallible sign of a heart inflamed by the Divine Spirit.[77]

> O highest grace! O gift than which nothing greater can be attained! What more wonderful benefits, favors, and charisms besides the Holy Spirit could the Lord impart to His disciples? He who possesses Him seems to have everything! He who is directed by Him cannot err, and a safe and straight road leads Him toward the heavenly Fatherland! As for you,

consider whether you have received the Holy Spirit today in the Most Holy Sacrament, whether you possess Him ... Know that these are the traits of the Holy Spirit: joy, peace, wisdom, gentleness, patience, humility, counsel, longanimity, and others like them (*see* Gal 5:22). If these do not shine forth from you, then not only do you not have the Holy Spirit, but not even a spark of the divine light.[78]

Points for personal prayer:

- Examine the action of the Holy Spirit in your life.
- Which of His gifts are present in me? How do I use them?
- What gifts do I particularly lack today? What gifts do I want to request?
- Invite the Holy Spirit and call upon Him with all His gifts.
- "O sevenfold Light, glide into our hearts, and dwell in them forever!"[79]

"Our five senses may not inappropriately be called the ministers of the Mystical Temple …. And so let us rather learn to seek God through the death of the senses, and we shall find him. They die, when they are directed wisely, when such things are removed from them by which brute animals themselves are attracted. Then, when the animal man dies, the spiritual one will arise, who, having found in himself God as his possession, will sweetly repeat with Paul: 'I live, no longer I, but Christ lives in me'" (Gal 2:20).

St. Stanislaus Papczyński

CHAPTER 6

The Sensory Ministers of the Temple[80]

"Our five senses may not inappropriately be called the ministers of the Mystical Temple."[81] Saint Stanislaus Papczyński dedicates separate chapters to two of them (sight and hearing), while writing briefly about the other three (touch, taste, and smell) in chapter 13. All the senses are meant to serve men, not lead them into the pitfalls of sin.

Before we delve into the teachings of our Saint, let's consider a passage from the Holy Scripture about the sin of David:

> At the turn of the year, at the time **when kings go campaigning**, David sent Joab and with him his guards and all Israel. They massacred the Ammonites and laid siege to Rabbah-of-the-Ammonites. **David, however, remained in Jerusalem.**
>
> **It happened towards evening when David had got up from resting** and was strolling on the palace roof, that from the roof he **saw a woman bathing**; the woman was very beautiful. David **made enquiries about this woman** and was told, "Why, that is Bathsheba, daughter of Eliam and **wife of Uriah** the Hittite." **David then sent messengers** to fetch her. **She came to him, and he lay with her,** just after she had purified herself from her period. She then went home again. **The woman conceived** and sent word to David, **"I am pregnant."**
>
> David then **sent word** to Joab, **"Send me Uriah the Hittite,"** whereupon Joab sent Uriah to David. When Uriah reached him, David asked how Joab was and how the army was and how the war was going.

David then said to Uriah, "Go down to your house and wash your feet." Uriah left the palace and was followed by a present from the king's table. Uriah, however, slept at the palace gate with all his master's bodyguard and did not go down to his house.

This was reported to David; "Uriah," they said, "has not gone down to his house." So David asked Uriah, "Haven't you just arrived from the journey? Why didn't you go down to your house?" To which Uriah replied, "The ark, Israel and Judah are lodged in huts; my master Joab and my lord's guards are camping in the open. Am I to go to my house, then, and eat and drink and sleep with my wife? As the LORD lives, and as you yourself live, I shall so no such thing!" David then said to Uriah, "Stay on here today; tomorrow I shall send you off." So Uriah stayed that day in Jerusalem. The next day, **David invited him to eat and drink in his presence and made him drunk.** In the evening, Uriah went out and bedded down with his master's bodyguard, but did not go down to his house.

Next morning **David wrote a letter to Joab and sent it** by Uriah. In the letter he wrote, **"Put Uriah out in front where the fighting is fiercest and then fall back, so that he gets wounded and killed."**

Joab, then besieging the city, stationed Uriah at a point where he knew that there would be tough fighters. The people of the city sallied out and engaged Joab; there were casualties in the army, among David's guards, and Uriah the Hittite was killed as well (2 Sam 11:1–17).

David's sin is not a single event but a kind of path, a progression of sin. It starts from what may seem like a small matter and leads to adultery and murder. It is worthwhile to trace the entire process of David's downfall to see in this story our own lapses, our journey from bad to worse.

"When kings go campaigning," David stayed in Jerusalem. We don't know if he was sick or if he just did not "feel like" going or if he found some good excuse to stay in his safe and comfortable palace instead of facing the hardships of the expedition. How many times do I stick to my activities when it is time for prayers, household chores, or unwanted tasks? It is worth presenting my excuses to God when, instead of fulfilling the duties that are required of me, I remain in my comfort zone, in my solitude, in my occupations. How do these excuses look before God?

One "evening," David got up from his bed. In the evening, we usually prepare for sleep rather than getting up from it. It appears that David doesn't know what to do with himself; he wanders around, seeking entertainment, satisfaction, something. From the terrace, he saw a woman bathing. He became interested in her. He inquired about her. He sent for her, even though he already knew she was married. These are the successive stages and actions on the path to a serious sin. As individual acts, they may seem insignificant and harmless. After all, maybe David just wanted to talk to her.

It is worth observing the growth of my sins, the process of drifting away from God. It's rare that anyone suddenly abandons God and their vocation (marriage, family, priesthood). It is more often a gradual process that ends in disaster. Men who abandon marriage or the priesthood usually start with innocent acquaintances. They then move on to friendships, meetings, increasingly frequent text messages, and closer contacts, until the final departure, which often occurs with a child or expecting one.

Bathsheba conceived and informed David of it. This is where another game of the king begins. To cover up one sin, a whole series of actions starts: summoning Uriah, inviting him to conversations and feasts at the palace, getting him drunk with wine. When everything failed, the decision came to kill the innocent Uriah. And it all started with staying at home and looking at the woman.

THE DOORS OF EYES

The doors of the temple are "the eyes," writes St. Stanislaus when recalling the story of David. "By a careless guarding of his eyes even that most just king David brought forth two monsters within the sanctuary of his mind: adultery and murder."[82]

Saint Stanislaus also mentions Eve, the mother of all the living. In her case, sin originated with the act of seeing that the fruits of the tree were fit to gain knowledge. In the words of scripture, "She saw ..." It's worth recalling the entire story of original sin described in the third chapter of Genesis.

Saint Stanislaus explains that as the doors of a physical temple serve for its protection and safety, so do the doors of the mystical temple. "For whatever is in the eyes is at once in the heart."[83] That is why "one sins unceasingly when these doors of the Mystical Temple are wide open everywhere and to everything."[84] Sin causes God to leave the temple: "As soon as anything base and evil flies into the soul through the eyes, at once Beauty and the Supreme Good fly away."[85]

It happens that someone watches very brutal, pornographic, satanic, or blasphemous films or plays video games and justifies it as "entertainment" or "seeing what people are into." However, such images penetrate and contaminate the heart. They remain in the imagination and carry further consequences and temptations.

Points for personal prayer:

- What do I gaze upon, what do my eyes behold?
- What do I most willingly view in both the real and virtual world? What images do I use my imagination for?
- What time or times do I want to set during the day to avoid letting any images from television, the internet, online messaging, etc., enter my inner self?
- What do my home and my room look like? What images or figurines are present?

- What could I change in the decor to lead me more towards God?

THE WINDOWS OF EARS

"Windows are ears," St. Stanislaus states briefly. When there is noise outside, we close the windows of the earthly temple to reduce distractions and devote ourselves more fully to prayer and communion with God.

In the case of ears, as in the case of eyes, there is a need for vigilance in seeking good conversations and words that bring God into our inner selves and defending ourselves against harmful conversations, judgments, gossip, and the like. Saint Stanislaus warns, "[Y]ou will be easily blackened if you lend an easy ear to all things."[86] It's worth repeating to ourselves that we are not a trash can into which any word or message can be thrown.

"Of course those ears are perfect which are open only to devout, salutary, virtuous and beneficial discourses; they are barred against those that are vain, prying, slanderous, licentious, hardly religious, not to say blasphemous."[87]

Saint Stanislaus' admonition sounds extremely contemporary: "Ah, wretched we are, while pious discourses and even sermons themselves weary us, we have taste of the things that are prying, fabled, harmful, detrimental."[88] Is it not strange that to relax after a hard day's work, some people listen to political debates, war reports, or crime chronicles? Other people immerse themselves in reading or listening to crime stories and all kinds of fiction, including literature that is very indecent, anti-God, and anti-Church. What benefit does this bring to my soul?

Saint Stanislaus quotes St. Paul's Letter to Timothy: "If you put all this to the brothers, you will be a good servant of Christ Jesus and show that you have really digested the teaching of the faith and the good doctrine which you have always followed. Have nothing to do with godless myths and old wives' tales" (1 Tim 4:6–7). Then St. Stanislaus adds that "we must avoid chatting, especially in the House of God, and especially at the time of a sermon."[89] Today it happens that, during Mass, people check and respond to text messages. Sometimes, a person leaves church to answer the phone or even answers it in the liturgical space. Is there really anyone important enough to interrupt our meeting with the Savior and the feast of His love?

"[W]e should not indeed present our ears to arguments and controversies that do not bring holiness and are not useful. Much more to be avoided are discourses and readings that not only lack any usefulness but also cause greatest harm."[90] When we engage in conversation, watch or listen to discussions and debates in the media, and read books, articles, and the news, we should always ask ourselves: Why am I doing this? What glorifies God in this? To what extent does this action bring me closer to God? To what extent does it distance me from Him? To what extent does it serve my spiritual life and my vocation to attain Heaven? Conversations, television broadcasts and programs, books, and everything that does me more harm than good should be calmly rejected, that the temple that I am may be full of God and entirely opposed to the devil.

Points for personal prayer:

- When do I have time reserved for reading or listening to God's Word, catechesis, homilies, and religious literature?
- What can or should I do about setting aside this time?
- What do my conversations sound like? To what extent do they serve my salvation and that of my companions and loved ones?
- What do I discuss and how do I discuss it? What benefit does this bring to me and others?
- To what extent do these conversations make me and my interlocutors better? To what extent do they poison my heart or arouse anger or doubt? What can I change in this regard? What should I change?

TOUCH

"**Touch**, if it performs its function properly, is of great service in advancing the beauty and strength of our Temple .... For we include under touch whatever our hands perform."[91] Saint Stanislaus considers touch and action to be good in regard to working honestly, reading books, writing works that are useful or serve salvation, giving alms, and completing acts of mercy. Touch is also good when our hands refrain from evil deeds or violence, when we make the Sign of the Cross, and when we control our bodies.

Touch is a true servant of the temple when it serves our soul and body, leading us to live a life even more dedicated to God. When writing about a good touch, St. Stanislaus refers to all the good deeds we perform with our hands and the evil deeds we refrain from. In conclusion, he adds, "Touch then is very beneficial and a most necessary minister for the Mystical Temple, provided it is on guard against what ought not to be touched."[92] Here, everyone can discover their own application for the principle of our Saint.

Points for personal prayer:

- Why do I complete some tasks and avoid others?
- What is the balance between work and rest?
- To what extent is it motivated by closeness and worship of God Himself?
- What touch, what deeds in my life turn me away from God?
- What do I intend to do about it?

TASTE

"**Taste** is settled in the mouth: therefore we can attribute to it whatever is done by the mouth."[93] Saint Stanislaus is primarily talking here about eating and drinking.

He emphasizes that we should "eat to live" and not "live to eat." He recommends avoiding overindulgence and excessive or overly-refined food. He also encourages avoiding a debauched life where eating and drinking are constant.

In calling for moderation in eating and drinking, the Marian Founder also promoted abstinence, particularly from strong alcohol. During his time, both the nobility and simple peasants often indulged in alcohol. The only difference was usually the type of drink they consumed. Strong alcohol, often heavily contaminated and intended for the lower classes, was referred to as *gorzałka* (burning vodka). It caused disease, poverty, and family suffering. That is why St. Stanislaus wrote in the *Rule of Life*: "Your ordinary drink ought to be water. Should you have any other drink, it will be up to the Superior to allow you to drink it sparingly, with the exception of vodka, which is absolutely prohibited to you."[94] His will on this topic is even more pronounced in another document: "Drinking of "burning vodka" [*crematum*] is forbidden both outside as well as inside the house under threat of losing the divine blessing, so as to honor Christ our Lord and Savior, [who was] thirsty upon the Cross."[95]

Today, fasting and abstaining from meat or limiting food for religious reasons are sometimes mocked or not taken seriously. Alcohol is often promoted as an integral part of relaxation at celebrations, sports events, or social gatherings. Simultaneously, new diets aimed at improving appearance and well-being are continuously emerging. Unfortunately, Poland, like many other countries, is witnessing a growing number of individuals struggling with alcohol and substance abuse issues.

Those who fast, for example, two to three times a week on bread and water or even just water, often do so "for the sake of Christ," relying on His power and grace. They undertake fasting and self-denial for their own sins, the sins of loved ones and the world, or for specific intentions. Many people voluntarily practice abstinence, seeking liberation from their own or others' addictions. Those who genuinely fast typically do not require a specific diet, because they maintain good health. Those who abstain enjoy freedom in their lives. What will you choose?

Ultimately, in the case of taste, as with all the senses, our goal is allowing taste in eating, and drinking to lead us to "bless and love" the One who provides us with "food and drink at the right time."

Points for personal prayer:

- What is the purpose of eating and drinking in my life?
- What forms of asceticism exist in my life?
- To what penance is God inviting me today?
- What is my level of alcohol consumption? What can I do to minimize it in my life and help others in this regard?
- What other dependencies do I see in myself (even in their very early stages)?
- What will I do to overcome any form of addiction in order to be free to live and love?

SMELL

"[The] proper task [of smell] is to prevent worthless smells."[96] Saint Stanislaus expresses some discomfort about those who anoint even their clothes, not just their tissues or gloves, with fragrances. He recognizes that various scents and perfumes can lead us astray, and, ultimately, this also concerns our salvation.

"Christians, I beg you, awaken your Smell, that is in so ugly a manner buried; awaken it; so that it may prevent worthless fragrance from the Temple of God, unless you wish to fall down or to be thrust down to where there is a hideous and everlasting stench."[97] Today, we not only anoint ourselves with perfumes but often use a variety of products and tools to make our bodies look younger and more beautiful. This applies not only to women but also to men. Today, St. Stanislaus would likely disapprove of this excessive concern for one's bodily appearance.

On the other hand, some should consider why they abstain from personal hygiene and avoid using any additional fragrances and "perfumes," leading to emitting odors that are unpleasant. When it comes to scents, we should take care of ourselves, but also consider others. Therefore, it would be worth asking whether we are attaching too little importance to our appearance and health.

Points for personal prayer:

- How does my care for my appearance and scent look? How much time and money do I dedicate to it?
- How does this compare to the time and energy I spend on prayer, reading the Word of God, and caring for my family?
- Care for my body can be excessive, but it can also be insufficient. Do I undergo regular check-ups? Do I take prescribed medications systematically? Do I maintain a healthy lifestyle?
- How much do I remember that I am a temple of the Holy Spirit and God's Tabernacle? Is the spiritual dimension of my life more important than the physical dimension? What can I use to assess this?

Ultimately, the author of *The Mystical Temple of God* encourages vigilance, mortification, and wise direction of the senses. Enlightened by faith, in our lives, the intellect should govern the senses, not the other way around. Animals follow their senses and are guided by them. When we can control our senses in a way that serves God and ourselves, rather than our passions, then "the animal man dies, [and] the spiritual one will arise, who, having found in himself God as his possession, will sweetly repeat with Paul: 'I live, no longer I, but Christ lives in me'" (Gal 2:20).[98] This is ultimately what Christianity is about: that I may die to self and let Christ reign within me.

Points for personal prayer:

- Once again, I can examine all my senses:
    - What do my eyes look at?
    - What do I listen to, and what do I close my ears to?
    - What do I occupy myself with in my life? What tasks do I perform, and what do I avoid?
    - What is my attitude toward eating and drinking? To what extent do they serve my life, and to what extent do they harm me and lead me to sin?
    - What is my concern for my own scent and the fragrances that surround me? Is it care for my appearance, my image, my health? Is this care excessive? Is it insufficient or contrary to self-love or love for my neighbor?
- What can or should I do to make my senses better serve the beauty of the temple that I am?
- What will I do in this matter?

> "Nor is it sufficient to apprehend the mere presence of God; we must also show in our actions and exterior deeds that we truly bear within us the living and unsullied image of God."
>
> St. Stanislaus Papczyński

CHAPTER 7

Take Care of Your Temple[99]

The temple that we are is holy and inhabited by God. His grace is given freely. "When we were still helpless, at the appointed time, Christ died for the godless" (Rom 5:6). "So it is proof of God's own love for us, that Christ died for us while we were still sinners" (Rom 5:8). We, by cooperating with God's grace, can make the mystical temple even more beautiful.

CONSCIENCE AS A PREACHER

During St. Stanislaus Papczyński's time, not every priest celebrating the Eucharist could preach sermons, and not everyone was allowed to teach. These ministries required specific knowledge confirmed by superiors. Therefore, in addition to the priest of love who offers the sacrifice on the altar of the heart, there is also a preacher in the mystical temple.

According to the Marian Founder, our conscience fulfills the role of preacher in the mystical temple. In his view, it is so zealous "that he is never dull," so strict "he never flatters," and so diligent "that he at once indicates and exposes our greatest and smallest defects, shows those which are to be corrected, and thunders against those which are to be avoided."[100]

Saint Stanislaus references the role of the conscience in the stories of Cain, Abimelech, and Joseph's brothers who sold him into Egypt (*see* Gen 4:6; Gen 26:28–29; Gen 43:18, respectively). You can select any of these stories and contemplate them anew using the commentary of St. Stanislaus.

For our conscience to responsibly fulfill the role of the preacher in our inner temple, it must be well-formed and continually nurtured. We also must allocate the appropriate time and space for a quiet examination of conscience (more about that in the next chapter) so that we can seriously engage with it every day.

"Happy is the man, who attends to this Advocate and obeys him. We would not need many books, nor most zealous preachers, if only we apply our mind to the whispers and voices of our conscience alone, and we would then commit nothing evil, nothing disgraceful and nothing abominable: but if committed, we would at once wash them out and return from our fall to grace with the God offended."[101]

Today, we often make excuses or find justifications for our sins: others do it too; other people do worse things than me; God is merciful and must forgive everything; I deserve something from life, etc. Saint Stanislaus was aware that the conscience can be corrupted, and, in such a state, it will not assist us much. "We have none closer to admonish us, and none more faithful, provided only that we do not corrupt it by choosing for ourselves teachers who tickle our ears" (cf. 2 Tim 4:3).[102] When we drift away from God and our calling, our conscience stirs unease within us. It is crucial to not silence it but to listen to what comes from within us, from the preacher in our temple, our conscience.

Saint Stanislaus adds that sometimes, "by pretense and dishonesty,"[103] we shape a deceitful conscience for ourselves: confession can be insincere; repentance rare and short-lived. Other times we have obedience without respect, prayer without intention, reading without attention and spiritual benefit, speech without prudence and restraint, etc. In all these cases, we seem to do good but without the proper intentions, without commitment, without reference to God and love. With a sick or deceitful conscience, we may not see our sin at all or attach too much importance to secondary matters. Therefore, we should ask God for a good conscience, shape it properly, and be attentive to its movements.

Saint Stanislaus concludes the chapter on conscience as the preacher with the following words: From deceitful and cunning conscience, "Free us, Lord …. For you do not judge by man's standards, but just as you know all things as they are done, so you judge. Therefore, implant upright judgment within me; give me an upright conscience and a ready and unchangeable will to obey my conscience."[104]

Points for personal prayer:

- How do I shape, care for, and use my conscience?
- When was the last time I heard the call of my conscience? What was this about?
- What times and spaces in my life are designated for listening to God and my conscience, through which God also speaks?
- Can I ask for guidance regarding my examinations of conscience? (instructions will be provided by St. Stanislaus in the next chapter.)
- Ask God for a good conscience properly used.

THE MUSIC OF EMOTIONS

Chapter 12 of *The Mystical Temple of God* is very beautiful. It speaks of the music of emotions, the symphony of feelings meant to praise God and lead us to Him. Today, we often fear various emotions: those considered negative, in order to not fall into sin, and those considered positive, to not violate Christian asceticism or temperance. Some people are accused of being constantly sad, while others of being constantly content and joyful.

Saint Stanislaus says, "In man the emotions take the place of music …. He who well tempers the emotions, praises God best with a harmonious symphony. … See, how beautifully all the emotions tend towards the one God, albeit by different paths, I should have said tones!"[105] The emotions are depicted here as singers and musicians meant to create wonderful music for the Lord.

By invoking various emotions, St. Stanislaus references passages from the Holy Scriptures, in which these emotions appear without judgment or rejection, always leading to greater unity with God. It is worth revisiting this little chapter frequently.

Saint Stanislaus quotes biblical passages that encompass love, sorrow, joy, sadness, hope, fear, desire, resignation, and gratitude. He continues to cite brief passages from the Word of God that can help those experiencing affliction, repentance, temptation, slander, persecution, and humiliation. "More examples of this kind can be drawn, both from the Psalms of David and diverse prayers of various saints,"[106] concludes St. Stanislaus.

Feelings are part of our humanity, not a random addition but meant to serve us. Our emotions help us to be more faithful to the Lord, more fervent and joyful, and more lovingly dedicated to our brothers and sisters. Life without feelings is "flattened." Without feelings, the Eucharist does not bring me joy, and sin does not sadden me.

If I see several people attacking a person and do not feel anger, compassion, or a sense of injustice, I will remain indifferent. Any feeling aroused by aggression towards another person can lead me to react: I can shout, take action, call the police, etc. Anger at injustice (for example, Russia's aggression against Ukraine) can lead me to actions to support the well-being of others. Joy and enthusiasm are powerful motivators for doing good. Sorrow over my own misery or disappointment in myself can lead me to abandon sin and cling more closely to God. Humiliation can make me more sensitive to another person and lead to forgiveness. Fear of harm being done to children can mobilize an alcoholic to fight addiction and prompt parents on the brink of divorce to make one more attempt at reconciliation.

However, it is still important for emotions to be guided by reason. Using the popular comparison that the body of a person is the carriage, emotions are the horses, and reason is the coachman, it is easy to understand that, without emotions, we will live in lethargy, not to say stagnation. Without reason, however, emotions will carry me wherever they want, often into the abyss of sin and self-destruction.

Emotions are necessary for a fuller, more "colorful," and intense life, a life closer to God. After all, He equipped us with emotions. However, they must be guided by reason. Here we could say that they are guided by the preacher-conscience, the lamps-commandments, and the seven-armed lampstand of the Holy Spirit and with His gifts.

Points for personal prayer:

- Which emotions do I fear to accept the most? Why?
- To what extent are my emotions guided by reason? To what extent do they govern everything?
- Which emotions bring me closest to the Lord?
- What can I do to make this true for all my emotions?
- To what extent do my emotions create a symphony in honor and praise of God?

ACTIONS AS A ROOF

"Temples are known by their roofs; in like manner a Christian is known by his works of righteousness, without which he is nothing but an empty name."[107]

Our actions either testify to the extent of our unity with Christ or to how much we are still walking the path of Satan and the world. To confirm the necessity of bearing witness to our faith through deeds, St. Stanislaus cites passages from the Gospels of Matthew and John, the Letter of St. John, and the Letters of St. Paul to Titus and the Ephesians. It is worthwhile to contemplate each of these passages from the Word of God or any of the following:

> You are salt for the earth. But if salt loses its taste, what can make it salty again? It is good for nothing, and can only be thrown out to be trampled under people's feet. You are light for the world. A city built on a hill-top cannot be hidden. No one lights a lamp to put it under a tub; they put it on the lamp-stand where it shines for everyone in the house. In the same way your light must shine in people's sight, so that, **seeing your good works, they may give praise** to your Father in heaven (Mt 5:13–16).

> This is what we have heard from him and are declaring to you: God is light, and there is no darkness in him at all. If we say that we share in God's life while

we are living in darkness, we are lying, because we are not living the truth. But if we **live in light**, as he is in light, we have a share in another's life, and the blood of Jesus, his Son, cleanses us from all sin (1 Jn 1:5–7).

In this way we know that we have come to know him, if we keep his commandments. Whoever says, "I know him" without keeping his commandments, is a liar, and truth has no place in him. But anyone who does keep his word, in such a one God's love truly reaches its perfection. This is the proof that we are in God. Whoever claims to remain in him must **act as he acted** (1 Jn 2:3–6).

No one who remains in him sins, and whoever sins has neither seen him nor recognized him. Children, do not let anyone lead you astray. Whoever acts uprightly is upright, just as he is upright. Whoever lives sinfully belongs to the devil, since the devil has been a sinner from the beginning. This was the purpose of the appearing of the Son of God, to undo the work of the devil. **No one who is a child of God sins** because God's seed remains in him. Nor can he sin, because he is a child of God (1 Jn 3:6–9).

How does it help, my brothers, when someone who has never done a single good act claims to have faith? Will that faith bring salvation? ... **faith, if good deeds do not go with it, is quite dead**. But someone may say: So you have faith and I have good deeds? Show me this faith of yours without deeds, then! It is by my deeds that I will show you my faith. You believe in the one God — that is creditable enough, but even the demons have the same belief, and they tremble with fear. ... You see now that it is by deeds, and not only by believing, that someone is justified. ... **As a body without a spirit is dead, so is faith without deeds** (Jas 2:14, 17–19, 24, 26).

Saint Stanislaus has no doubt that our deeds clearly reveal whether we have the Holy Spirit or other spirits. "Do you say, or at least believe, that you have the Holy Spirit? The roof shows me what guest lives inside."[108] Whoever is greedy, proud, dissolute, angry, gluttonous, envious, sluggish, St. Stanislaus says, has no Holy Spirit within him.

He states: "He therefore that does good is recognized to be the Temple of God; he that does evil is a chapel of the devil."[109] At the end of chapter 17 of *The Mystical Temple of God* he adds, "Let us therefore prove our faith by works of faith, since by means of these roofs we both are and are acknowledged to be the Temples of the living God."[110]

Points for personal prayer:

- To what does the roof of my temple, my deeds, testify?
- When am I a temple of God, and when am I a chapel of the devil?
- What are my most serious sins resulting from disbelief and lack of trust in God?
- Looking at my life, do people approach to God, or do they withdraw from Him?
- Does it concern me at all?
- What can I change in this matter?

FAME AS A BELL

The bell of the temple, according to St. Stanislaus, is a person's glory. He recommends taking care of our good name, even defending it if it is attacked unjustly, because the glory of a Christian brings glory to God Himself, the Creator and Inhabitant of the mystical temple.

"Although the sound of reputation should be attended to rather seldom, since it increases or decreases in accordance with men's feelings, and nobody should be immediately considered worthless on the basis of popular bias, yet every servant and follower of Jesus Christ should strive to procure for himself a good name among all, as far as he is able."[111] This is in line with the teachings of the Holy Scriptures: "Fame is preferable to great wealth, favor, to silver and gold" (Prov 22:1). "Better a good name than costly oil, the day of death than the day of birth" (Eccl 7:1).

Of course, the goal is not to maintain a good reputation while living in wickedness but for it to arise from a good life. "A truly good name is one that is advanced, nurtured, and maintained by a good life, virtue, integrity, genuine devotion, constant zeal for God's glory, a true contempt for human affairs, concern for eternal things, love of God, love of neighbor, a conduct adapted to Divine perfections, the same disposition in adversities and in prosperity, and particularly conserved by those greatest sources of all the virtues, faith, hope, and charity."[112] At the end of the chapter about the bell of the mystical temple, St. Stanislaus adds, "Finally the best means to win and keep a good name is as follows: slander nobody, do not listen to those who do so, do not be grudging in your praises of others."[113] This is the kind of good behavior which is similar to those included in the letters of St. Paul the Apostle, among others.

Saint Stanislaus emphasizes that if someone wanted to destroy our reputation or good name, "You will be able, indeed you shall be obliged, to boldly rise against"[114] them. He continues that this course of action consists in not allowing falsehood to spread, thus preventing harm to those who would be deceived by error or falsehood. In the biography of St. Stanislaus, we find events where he defended his good name before ecclesiastical and secular courts (for example, against the Piarists and the residents of Marianki in New Jerusalem).

In our times, the unjust accusation against the late Cardinal George Pell in Australia is a notable example. He subjected himself to all legal procedures, spent a considerable time in prison, and was ultimately acquitted when the accusations were proven false. This was important not only for his good name but also for the Church, which is often falsely accused. Such false accusations can lead people to turn away from the Church or even become its adversaries. In some cases, defending the Church's reputation or our own is necessary to prevent the spread of falsehood or manipulation.

Saint Stanislaus advises not to respond to light slander with severe punishment. He suggests that we should have no reaction in matters of little importance. Ultimately, even Christ Himself was judged and slandered in various ways, yet He often did not respond to minor attacks. Therefore, St. Stanislaus encourages us to follow the example of St. Paul by focusing more on pursuing a virtuous life than caring about human opinions. "Am I trying to please human beings? If I were still doing that I should not be a servant of Christ" (Gal 1:10).

Saint Stanislaus assures us that by living a virtuous life according to God's plan, we will gain and maintain a good reputation and name. In this way, the bell of the mystical temple of God will ring clearly and loudly.

Points for personal prayer:

- What reputation do I enjoy among people?
- To what extent does my life proclaim the glory of the Lord?
- How do I care for my good name?
- Do I endure small humiliations and slander without defending myself against them?
- Ask God for wisdom and strength in order to discern when to fight defamation and when to allow my name to be tarnished, so that my actions will be of God.

VIRTUES AS ORNAMENTS

"Virtue is the principle ornament of a Christian."[115] What St. Stanislaus considered evident is often ridiculed today. Speaking about cultivating virtue or living a virtuous life may seem out of date to many, childish or unworthy of "reasonable, mature, or open Christianity." Virtuous and good living is mocked even more by contemporary culture and society.

Saint Stanislaus assures us that God Himself adorns us with beautiful garments, namely natural and supernatural virtues. First, he clothes us with theological virtues (faith, hope, and charity), "since without them eternal salvation cannot be obtained."[116] "It is impossible to please God without faith" (Heb 11:6) and "a hope which will not let us down, because the love of God has been poured into our hearts by the Holy Spirit which has been given to us" (Rom 5:5). We are adorned with faith and hope in this earthly life, he emphasized, while the brilliance of love will be preserved in Heaven for those who are saved.

Saint Stanislaus comments on the hymn about love (1 Cor 13:1–7) and explains that many different virtues are encompassed within the image of love. Referring to St. Bernard and St. Macarius, he lists as virtues qualities such as mercy, truth, justice, peace, purity, patience, humility, prudence, and more. He also asserts that both virtues and vices are interconnected, mutually dependent, and form chains of virtues or vices. Among vices, he mentions actions like hatred, anger, pride, infidelity, hardness of heart, negligence, laziness, indifference, impatience, sensuality, and more.

God grants us various virtues to guard, instruct, guide, and protect us. Although virtues are gifts from God to adorn our temple, we also have a responsibility to nurture these virtues and combat our vices. We should use virtues to attain the love of God, our own salvation, and the salvation of our brethren.

At the end of his reflection on virtues, the adornments of the mystical temple, St. Stanislaus returns to love as the keystone and safeguard of all other virtues. After all, love serves as the priest in the mystical temple of God. "For unless the virtues are practiced from the love of God, they have no merit before God. Love endows them with value and splendor just as they do so for the Mystical Temple."[117]

It is worth recalling St. Paul's entire hymn about love, and reading and meditating on it repeatedly. It is also valuable to accept it as the program of my life, desire, and future:

Though I command languages both human and angelic — if I speak without love, I am no more than a gong booming or a cymbal clashing. And though I have the power of prophecy, to penetrate all mysteries and knowledge, and though I have all the faith necessary to move mountains — if I am without love, I am nothing. Though I should give away to the poor all that I possess, and even give up my body to be burned — if I am without love, it will do me no good whatever.

Love is always patient and kind; love is never jealous; love is not boastful or conceited, it is never rude and never seeks its own advantage, it does not take offence or store up grievances. Love does not rejoice at wrongdoing, but finds its joy in the truth. It is always ready to make allowances, to trust, to hope and to endure whatever comes. Love never comes to an end. But if there are prophecies, they will be done away with; if tongues, they will fall silent; and if knowledge, it will be done away with. For we know only imperfectly, and we prophesy imperfectly; but once perfection comes, all imperfect things will be done away with.

When I was a child, I used to talk like a child, and see things as a child does, and think like a child; but now that I have become an adult, I have finished with all childish ways. Now we see only reflections in a mirror, mere riddles, but then we shall be seeing face to face. Now I can know only imperfectly; but then I shall know just as fully as I am myself known.

As it is, these remain: faith, hope and love, the three of them; and the greatest of them is love. (1 Cor 13:1–13).

Points for personal prayer:

- What virtues do I observe in myself today?
- Where do I see faith, hope, and love within myself?
- Which virtues should I particularly develop? How?
- What are the most serious faults I notice in myself? How did they develop?
- How do I intend to fight against them?

"Examination of one's conscience:
the more frequently and diligently it is used,
the cleaner it makes the dwelling place of
God in man. The Reconciliation of
[the original sanctity received in Baptism]
of the Mystical Temple takes place in
Penance and in Holy Communion."

St. Stanislaus Papczyński

CHAPTER 8

Cleaning and Reconciliation[118]

The mystical temple of God, which we are, is constantly polluted by our sins. With mortal sins, it even becomes desecrated and desacralized, as St. Stanislaus Papczyński describes, quoting another saint, "a habitation of darkness, a repository of the devil."[119] However, God does not leave us without hope. We can daily cleanse the temple through an examination of conscience, and it is reconsecrated when we submit to the Sacraments of Penance/Reconciliation and the Eucharist.

CLEANING THROUGH EXAMINATIONS OF CONSCIENCE

"Cleanliness is greatest if the temple is swept out at least once a day. ... This is done by the examination of one's conscience: the more frequently and diligently it is used, the cleaner it makes the dwelling place of God in man."[120]

Saint Stanislaus recommends frequent examination of conscience, "at least every evening."[121] During the day, it can be more challenging to find the time and proper focus, so the evening can be the best moment for it.

Saint Stanislaus, the Prophet of the Immaculate Conception, cries out in disappointment, "O Christian! Every day you wash your face, every day you clean your clothes, every day you sweep out your house, so why do you not do this every day with the Temple of God, which you are."[122] With cleaning the house, we might not be that meticulous, but when it comes to washing our face or general personal hygiene — certainly yes. He is also surprised that the same people who cannot stand dirty rooms, clothing, dishes, or utensils have no problem with the impurity of their own hearts. They take care of their bodies daily but completely neglect the purity of their souls. Today, we could add: O Christian! You, who constantly scroll through your smartphone and check your email and online news several times a day, who read and send dozens of different messages and notifications every day — why do you reflect so rarely on your own life?

Saint Stanislaus recommends examining three areas: thoughts, words, and actions. We should not only ask ourselves about sins, what we thought, said, or did, but also about how we could have done things better. What was our intention? Did we miss an opportunity to do good? These questions and the entire examination of conscience should ultimately lead us to transform our hearts and lives, achieve a greater love for God and our neighbors, and more ardently pursue good.

According to the verse known in the time of our Saint, he recommends an examination of conscience consisting of six points: "Thank God, ask for light, examine your mind, ask pardon for sin, and resolve, make satisfaction."[123]

It is worth rediscovering the daily examination of conscience and practicing it with greater zeal. It is a powerful aid on the path toward repentance and transformation of life. Saint Ignatius of Loyola used to say that a neglected meditation is a lesser evil than an abandoned examination of conscience. In the examination of conscience, we most effectively correct our lives and align them with Christ's example.

It may sometimes seem that we no longer have time for anything additional, especially the examination of conscience. However, through the examination, we can abandon unnecessary actions and do others in a new, better way. We can also manage our day differently and discover new insights.

Thanksgiving. In his examination of conscience, St. Stanislaus recommends starting with thanksgiving (similarly to what St. Ignatius of Loyola advised earlier). Thanksgiving is an excellent tool to overcome bitterness, complaining, or envy. God desired me before the foundation of the world, loved me, called me into existence, and prepared me to be happy for all eternity. He continually bestows gifts upon me because I am His beloved child.

Saint Stanislaus recommends beginning our thanksgiving in a general way, by thanking God for the blessings and graces granted to me and all of humanity from the beginning of the world until today. Then our thanksgiving should become more individual, by expressing gratitude for the graces granted to me in particular: creation and redemption, being called to the Catholic faith, insights, the gift of conversion. You can also thank God for your parents, ancestors, family, and friends; for those who passed on the faith to you; for the Sacraments and those who administer them; and for your vocation to marriage, religious life, or the priesthood. You can also express thankfulness for everything that the Holy Spirit prompts you to see, revealing to you how much you have been gifted and guided from the beginning of your life through its entire history.

Finally, you should reach a point of thanksgiving for the gifts received today, the people you've met, the experiences you've had, the tasks you've completed.

Thanksgiving should transition from the general to the specific, from the world to my particular life, from eternity to today. It is valuable to conclude thanksgiving by blessing and glorifying God in all His gifts and works, especially in myself, in my thoughts, words, and deeds.

The request for light. Saint Stanislaus cites a short, clear prayer that should be developed anew each time: "Enlighten, Lord, the eyes of my mind, that I may acknowledge Your good deeds and my evil deeds: may I bless You for the former, and weep over the latter and amend them with Your grace for your glory. Amen."[124]

Therefore, a daily examination does not just consist in counting sins or accusing or condemning myself. Instead, I should ask for light, that I may recognize God's blessings and my failures, worship God, and, through His grace, transform my life, in order that everything I have and do may further the glory of God and the salvation of myself and my brothers.

The Holy Spirit's role is particularly significant in the examination, and we should constantly invoke Him. Jesus promised, "I shall ask the Father, and he will give you another Paraclete to be with you for ever, the Spirit of truth .... the Paraclete, the Holy Spirit, whom the Father will send in my name, will teach you everything and remind you of all I have said to you"

(Jn 14:16–17, 26). "[U]nless I go, the Paraclete will not come to you; but if I go, I will send him to you. And when he comes, he will show the world how wrong it was, about sin, and about who was in the right, and about judgement" (Jn 16:7–8).

The request for light is a cry for the Holy Spirit, so that I may see God's love and my wrongdoing, confess my sins, and worship God. It is also a request for me to recognize my sins and experience God's mercy.

Examination of conscience. Only in the third point should I review the thoughts, words, and actions since my last examination of conscience to identify those that were contrary to God's will, times when I followed the promptings of the devil, the world, or the flesh, rather than the light of the Holy Spirit. The criteria for assessment should be love, God's commandments, natural and Church law, and human laws.

When, in the evening examination, I calmly reflect on the day just ending, I can see the people I hurt with my words or actions. Even if they gave me some sign of my wrongdoing, I rushed to the next task. I can recall the people I lied to or deceived at work or in the shop. I can see the time that slipped through my fingers, which I could have used better. If I do not stop in the evening to reflect on my day, all the events will merge into one, and I will continue to do the evil to which I have become accustomed.

When I see actions contrary to God, His love, or love for my neighbor, I should further examine in my conscience, arouse remorse, and submit myself to God's mercy. This examination is also a preparation for the next confession, which in the case of mortal sins should be as soon as possible.

Remorse for sins. Having discovered faults or transgressions in my conscience, I ask God to grant me genuine remorse for them and all my sins in general. Saint Stanislaus provides an example of expressing remorse for sins that can be used directly or developed in one's own words.

Remorse for sins should primarily originate from pure love for God, not because of discomfort, disappointment in myself, or humiliation experienced. Remorse for sins committed recently should lead to remorse for all my sins. From remorse for my sins, I can also advance to remorse for the sins of others and the whole world. Remorse for sins ends with requesting forgiveness of all evil committed by me and by other people, not because of my good deeds or prayers, but because of the merits of Jesus Christ, Mary, and all the saints.

The structure of expressing remorse for sins proposed by St. Stanislaus is beautiful and wise. It is worth modifying it according to our needs, depending on our particular state and the Holy Spirit's inspiration.

Resolution for improvement. Here, once again, St. Stanislaus suggests a specific prayer: a cry to God, Who is goodness and love itself, and a desire and declaration of loving God above all else.

In the resolution for improvement, it is worth considering and planning how to change our bad behavior. A mere declaration of intent is not enough. If you desire more prayer, Scripture reading, or adoration of the Blessed Sacrament, you should plan specific times and places during the week for these activities. If being in a particular company (at work, school, family, or in a shop) always ends in gossiping and talking behind other people's backs, and you cannot change it, you should discontinue such relationships. If meeting with certain people always ends in excessive drinking or arguments, avoid such gatherings. If you always arrive late for Mass, plan a different schedule for leaving home, and so on. Things do not change on their own.

Before God, Saint Stanislaus expresses his desire to love God above all things and for God to be loved by all people as He deserves. He prays that the human response to God's love may be as adequate and fitting as possible, in accordance with the love that God bestows upon us. Finally, he declares the intention to purify oneself from sins through Confession, improve through God's grace, and make reparation for sins.

Indeed, starting from the mystery of the Immaculate Conception, in resolving to amend our lives, it is valuable to not only ask God for the grace of rising from sin but also for the grace of not sinning at all, in order that we may be holy and unblemished. God, Who can lift us and cleanse us from sin, can also keep us from sin.

Lord, grant that I may no longer sin! May I be entirely devoted to You today and always.

Atonement. Depending on the sins committed, St. Stanislaus proposes atonement, such as mortification, prayer, almsgiving, and fasting, as "the quality and magnitude of the sin demands, and as the Spirit of God teaches you. Thus you will clean the Temple of God, and so you will advance in His grace, love, and perfection."[125]

Atonement should not be just a light, formal act or hastily recited prayer; it should lead me to grow in God's grace and perfection. I should also think about what I can do specifically for the people I have hurt or scandalized with my sin. How will I make amends to those I slandered, deceived, or robbed? Stolen items should be returned, damaged things repaired, false accusations withdrawn, sharp treatment apologized for, and reconciliation sought from those with whom I quarrelled. Atonement is a concrete action, commensurate with sin, sometimes very difficult and painful. It is not just a lofty statement made in private.

Finally, St. Stanislaus encourages us, "[H]aving become better by his admonition, cleanse your soul every day by a strict examination; in this way it will be a dwelling pleasing to God forever."[126]

In the chapter about cleaning the temple, St. Stanislaus is incredibly specific and clear. The entire process of cleansing — the examination of conscience — can be applied right away or modified and expanded according to one's needs. It is a very effective prayer. When practiced diligently every day, it yields great spiritual benefits.

Points for personal prayer:

- What does my daily examination of conscience look like?
- What hinders me from practicing it? What can I do to make it a permanent part of my life?
- What place do thanksgiving and worship of God have in my prayer?

- Do I invite the Holy Spirit into my life and ask for His gift of discernment?
- How do I recognize and repent for my sins?
- What does my resolution for improvement look like?
- To what extent do I make amends to God and others?
- What have I done recently for the people I have hurt with my sins?

RESTORING THE ORIGINAL HOLINESS

"This takes place in Penance and in Holy Communion. For when the Temple of God that we are is polluted by sins, especially mortal ones, ... [for] the Reconciliation [of this temple] these two **Sacraments of Penance and Eucharist** were established by Jesus Christ."[127]

Penance, according to St. Stanislaus, is "a kind of second Baptism."[128] He explains, "Penance is fitting both to a virtue of this kind and the Sacrament." [129] Although recognizing the power of penance as a virtue, St. Stanislaus explains that "the power of the Sacrament is greater, by which sanctifying grace is properly conferred unless some obstacle is placed before it on the part of the penitent."[130]

The Saint recommends preparing for the Sacrament of Penance and Reconciliation by almsgiving, fasting, and mortification to allow God to grant the penitent knowledge of his or her sins, proper contrition, and a "salutary confession."

According to St. Stanislaus, **the examination of conscience** should be preceded by a short prayer. For this one should find a suitable place away from any witnesses. You should carefully examine your thoughts, words, and actions according to the method of the daily examination of conscience mentioned above (chapter 16 on purifying the temple). Consider the commandments of God and the Church, civil laws, your vocation, and your state in life: virginity, marriage, widowhood, singleness, religious life, or the priesthood. Ultimately, your "conscience itself ... will show what one should grieve over, confess, and censure."[131]

Remorse for sin should encompass all sins, both general and specific, particularly mortal sins, and lead to **a resolution to amend ourselves.** The words of St. Stanislaus are remarkably wise in this regard. "This [remorse] does not consist so much in feelings and tears, even though these are good and most pleasing to God, as in the acts of judgment and understanding, by which the gravity of a sin is understood, which results from having offended the Supreme Good."[132]

Sometimes people wonder what to do if they lack feelings of remorse for what their conscience or the Church calls a sin. This usually pertains to the feeling of remorse. Saint Stanislaus hastens to explain that if a penitent lacks the appropriate remorse and resolution to amend his or her life, especially if attached to a particular sin frequently committed, this person should humbly ask God for the gift of true remorse. He should ask for remorse of his intellect and will, rather than of feelings, petitioning God for the desire to rise from sin and to sin no more! People in this state should ask for the strengthening of the will so that they may reject all sin and desire it no more!

The confession of sins should be done humbly, sincerely, and courageously (without concealing or omitting anything), with the inclusion of relevant circumstances, without diminishing sins or making excuses. Saint Stanislaus reminds us that the penitent "is confessing not to man but to God, to whom all that is inside of every man is very well known, and to whom sins are known before anyone commits them."[133]

Saint Stanislaus recommends that you listen to and implement the guidance and instructions of the confessor with humility, and in humility accept the penance imposed, and promptly fulfill it. He suggests that you add something more on your own initiative and fulfill the conditions for obtaining indulgences. It sometimes occurs that someone comes to confession after a long time and cannot remember what penance they were given or whether they completed it. Thus a good practice is to fulfill the confessor's orders as soon as possible, even adding something more to it.

In all of St. Stanislaus' advice, you can feel his pastoral experience, sensitivity to the Holy Spirit, and concern for his fellow Christians. All his recommendations can serve us well individually. His advice can also assist those for whom we are responsible in various ways before God. It is worth reflecting on the quality of our confessions and making appropriate resolutions according to his guidance.

The parable of the prodigal son (Lk 15:11–32) beautifully illustrates the essence of confession. The younger son, who had squandered his father's wealth and lived recklessly, becomes a servant to others. Finally, he returns home hungry and suffering and confesses his sins to his father, both those against him and against God. The father, who eagerly awaits him, joyfully embraces him, clothes him in a new robe as a sign of restored sonship, a ring as a sign of inheritance, and sandals as the sign of a free man. Then he invites his son to a feast, which symbolizes the Eucharist.

This is what happens to us during the Sacrament of Penance/Reconciliation. When we come in contrition, God the Father throws His arms around us and restores our lost dignity and inheritance. He consecrates us anew and invites us to the feast of the Eucharist, that we may partake of the Body and Blood of Christ, the nourishment for eternal life. The priest sitting in the confessional is an instrument of the merciful God, a dispenser of mercy. Even if he is having a bad day or hurts us with some word or gesture, God still holds us in His arms and sanctifies us anew. All we need to do to receive this is to confess our sins, experience remorse for them, resolve to change, and perform acts of penance.

It is best to go to confession immediately when you realize that you have committed a mortal sin. Mortal sins can be defined as serious offences against the love of God, humanity, or oneself, committed with full awareness and freedom. For example, deliberately skipping Sunday Mass out of laziness, social engagements, sporting interests, etc., can be considered a mortal sin. However, it is not a sin to miss Mass due to being in the hospital or providing necessary care for a sick child, elderly person, or someone else in need. God does not demand the impossible from us. Mortal sins involve serious violations of God's commandments but do not include actions committed in dreams (because of a lack of free will) or under duress.

It is also a worthwhile practice to go to confession when your conscience doesn't accuse you of any specific mortal sin, but you feel burdened by an accumulation of venial sins and various neglects that seem to separate you from God. It is a good practice to go to confession every month. During this time, you can reflect on the past month and surrender it to God's mercy. Especially if you don't regularly examine your conscience, there might be longer intervals between confessions. However, this makes it difficult to see and assess your real life. In such cases, you may tend to confess sins that have become habitual and have been with you for a long time.

The Eucharist holds a central place in the teachings of St. Stanislaus. He saw it as the source of life, forgiveness of sins, and conversion. The Second Vatican Council declared that the Eucharist is the summit toward which the entire activity of the Church is directed and the source from which all its power flows. We can say that the Prophet of the Immaculate Conception lived according to this principle in his congregation almost 300 years before the Council.

Most of St. Stanislaus' book *Examination of the Heart* consists of meditations for every Sunday, feast day, and liturgical celebration throughout the year. Each meditation is prepared to help readers better experience the Mass and contains three points to prepare for the reception of Holy Communion and three points for thanksgiving and strengthening in goodness after Communion. All of these meditations are based on the liturgical readings and the Scriptures. The Eucharist with Holy Communion is undoubtedly a source of life for sinners and the most intimate and fruitful encounter with God.

In *The Mystical Temple of God*, St. Stanislaus reminds us that in the Eucharist, on one hand, we come to the Almighty God, and on the other hand, "because He is of unbounded goodness, He not only kindly waits for you, but — what is more — calls you to Himself, so that He may cleanse and sanctify your inner being by the sharing of Himself."[134]

Therefore, St. Stanislaus recommends receiving Communion frequently, always worthily and in a state of grace. He assures us that the martyrs of the early centuries had the readiness and strength for martyrdom because they often received Communion. In the early days of the Marian Congregation, the 17th century, Christians went to confession more often than to Communion. Many people, as a rule, received Communion only once a year. Various Church confraternities allowed their members to increase this frequency usually to a few times a year. In encouraging frequent Communion, St. Stanislaus recalls the words of Christ Himself: whoever partakes of the Body of Christ "will live for ever" (Jn 6:58).

Saint Stanislaus, quoting St. Cyril, enlightens sinners, saying, "Do you suffer from pride? Receive the Eucharist, that is, Christ humiliating Himself down to flesh, indeed down to bread, and this humble bread will make you humble. Are you afflicted with temptation of lust? Receive the wine that generates virgins. Are you afflicted with anger and impatience? Receive Christ the crucified, the most patient, He will give you a share in His patience."[135] For all needs, desires, and sufferings, the Eucharist is undoubtedly the most powerful remedy and support. Here, Christ gives Himself to us in His Body and Blood. Whoever receives Him "has eternal life" — a life available to us today.

Chapter 22 of *The Mystical Temple,* which focuses on the restoration of the original holiness of the temple, concludes with a prayer inspired by the writings of St. Augustine, titled "The invocation of Almighty God for the reform of our morals and life." This beautiful text invokes God the Father, Creator, Savior, King, Ruler, and Mercy Itself to help us rise from our sins and avoid falling into them again, conquer our faults, and develop virtues. It is a very beautiful prayer in the spirituality of the Immaculate Conception of the Blessed Virgin Mary, suitable for all times. It can serve as a closing prayer for meditation and as an examination of conscience, especially for those who may not readily recognize their sins:

> O Lord my God! Bestow desire upon my heart, that
> I may desire you; that by desiring You, I may seek

You; that by seeking You, I may find You; that by finding You I may love You, that by loving You, I may be freed from all my sins; and that once being freed, I may return to them no more.

O Lord my God! Grant repentance to my heart, contrition to my spirit, a fountain of tears to my eyes, and liberality in giving alms, to my hands.

O my King! Extinguish all desires of the flesh and kindle the fire of Your love in me.

O You my Redeemer, drive away the spirit of pride; and grant me, through Your mercy, the treasure of Your humility.

O You, my Savior! Remove from me the fury of anger and vouchsafe me (of Your grace) the shield of patience.

O You my Creator! Take all rancor from me; and through Your meekness, enrich me with a sweet and gentle mind.

Bestow on me, O most merciful Father, a solid faith, a suitable hope, and continual charity!

O You my Director! Remove from me vanity and inconstancy of mind, unsettledness of heart, scurrility of speech, pride of eyes, gluttony of diet, the offense of my neighbors, the wickedness of detractions, the itch of curiosity, the desire for riches, the seizure of powers, the ambition for vainglory, the mischief of hypocrisy, the poison of flattery, the contempt for the poor, the oppression of the weak, the eagerness of covetousness, the rottenness of envy, and a death-causing blasphemy.

Cut away from me, O You who are my Maker, heedlessness, wickedness, pertinacity, unquietness, idleness, somnolence, sloth, dullness of mind, blindness of heart, obstinacy of judgment, crudeness of conduct, refractoriness of the good, resistance to advice, imprudence of speech, plunder of the poor, violence inflicted upon the impotent, false accusation of the innocent, negligence of the subjects, severity towards the members of the household, irresponsibility towards the members of the family, hardness towards neighbors.

O my God and my mercy, I beseech You through Your beloved Son, grant that I may perform the works of mercy, grant me the inclinations of devotion; suffering with the afflicted, advising those that err, comforting the miserable, aiding those in want, consoling those in sorrow, relieving the oppressed, refreshing the poor, refreshing the tearful; forgiving those who trespass against me, pardoning those who do me wrong, loving those who hate me, rendering good for evil, despising nobody, but honoring all, imitating the good, guarding against the bad, embracing virtues, rejecting vices, having patience in adversity, and moderation in prosperity; setting a guard at my mouth, and shutting the door of my lips: despising earthly things, and thirsting for heavenly ones ... Amen.[136]

Points for personal prayer:

- How do I prepare for the Sacrament of Penance/Reconciliation?
- What is my usual frequency of confession? Do I choose peaceful times when there are fewer people, or do I wait for retreats or holidays when confession is very quick due to the large number of penitents?
- How do I prepare for the Eucharist and thank God afterwards?
- What do I desire when receiving the Body and Blood of Christ? What do I ask for? What am I waiting for?

- To what extent are the Eucharist and Holy Communion the center of my life? To what extent do they transform and shape me?
- What can I do to make the Eucharist more fruitful in my life?

"The Mystical Temple is brought to ruin by impious deeds and repaired by pious deeds. … For mercy embracing everything is able both to appease the angry God and to retain the grace of the favorable God. There are fourteen works of mercy by which you will achieve everything with God."

St. Stanislaus Papczyński

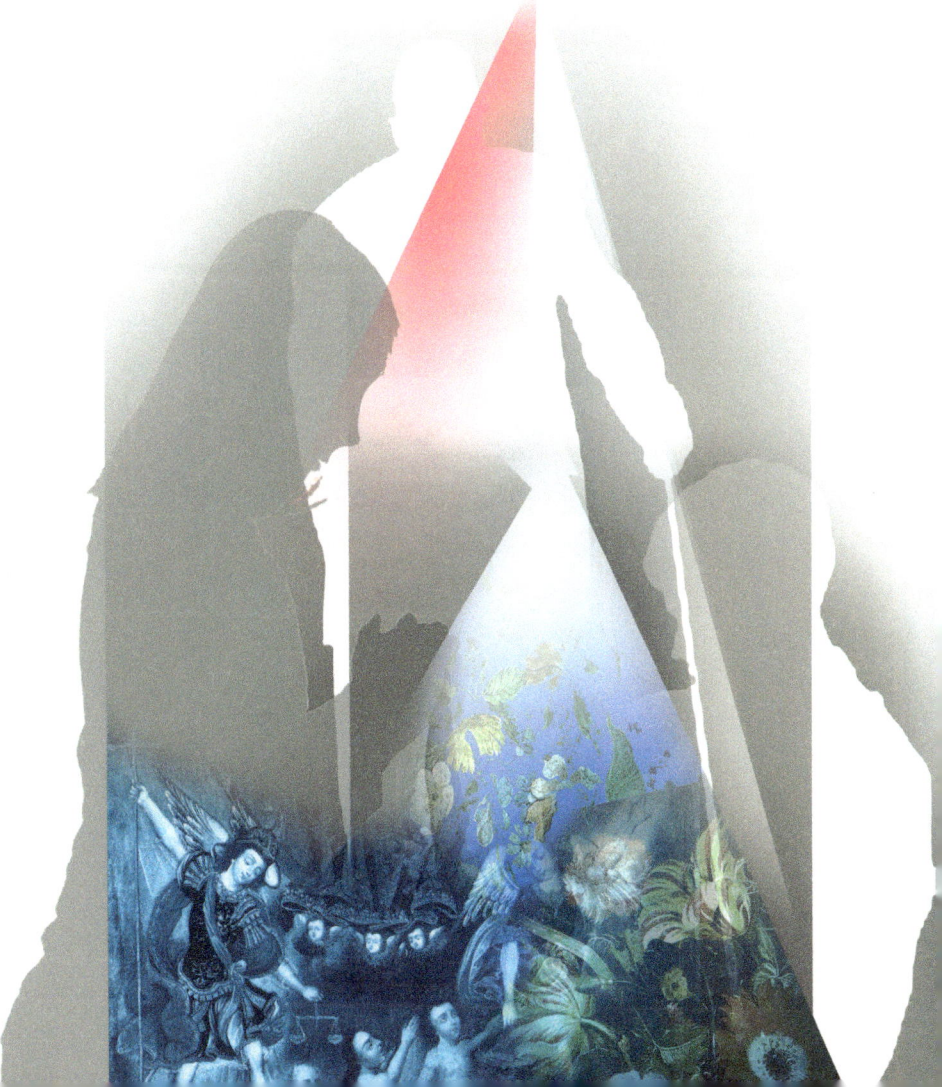

CHAPTER 9
Restoration[137]

Chapter 21 of *The Mystical Temple of God*, "The Restoration of the Mystical Temple," is the longest in the book. In the edition we use, the entire text of *The Mystical Temple of God* spans 98 pages, divided into 24 chapters. Chapter 21 occupies 15 pages, one-seventh of the entire book.

"The Mystical Temple is brought to ruin by impious deeds and repaired by pious deeds. ... For mercy embracing everything is able both to appease the angry God and to retain the grace of the favorable God. There are fourteen works of mercy by which you will achieve everything with God."[138]

What St. Stanislaus Papczyński refers to as pious deeds, we now call works of mercy for the soul and body. He lists in Latin hexameter seven acts related to the body and seven related to the soul. Those related to the body can be translated as follows: "I visit, give drink, give food, ransom, clothe, take in, bury."[139] Those regarding the soul can be translated as "I advise, forgive, console, admonish, teach, pray, remit."[140]

Saint Stanislaus describes most of the 14 pious deeds in great detail, making it sometimes heavy, but highly practical, reading. Here, I will present them briefly. It is worth remembering that, according to St. Stanislaus, while these acts benefit our fellow man, they also renew the temple of ourselves and can "appease the angry God and to retain the grace of the favorable God."

Saint Stanislaus provides justification and encouragement for each of these acts by citing passages from the Holy Scripture and facts from the lives of the saints. When reviewing all these acts, it is worth considering to what extent they exist and function in my life, the life of my family, or my community. What could I improve in this matter?

CORPORAL ACTS OF MERCY

Act 1: Visiting the Sick.

"*Visiting the sick* is praised by our Lord and Savior Himself, who said, '[I was sick], and you visited me'" (Mt 25:36).[141]

In the *Rule of Life,* St. Stanislaus instructed the Marian Fathers to care for their sick brethren and provide them with companionship. He himself cared for and visited the sick, and many were healed through his intercession. Even today, when asked for his intercession, he obtains healing for many people, in both soul and body.

Upon receiving the most recently printed edition of *Rycerz Niepokalanej* (The Knight of the Immaculate), St. Maximilian Kolbe used to go first to the hospice in Niepokalanów, Poland, where they took care of the sick and the oldest Franciscans. He told them, "We have done everything we can; the rest depends on your prayers." He had a great appreciation for the sick and suffering, recognizing the value of their suffering and prayer.

I can ask myself:

- How do I experience my illnesses?
- Am I able to ask for help when I need it?
- Am I taking advantage of others when I could manage on my own?
- Am I grateful to those who care for me and provide help, such as my doctors, nurses, family, friends?
- Do I pray for them?
- How am I a source of support for the sick and elderly, such as my elderly parents or siblings, friends, and acquaintances?

Acts 2 and 3: Providing food and drink to those in need.

Saint Stanislaus, citing examples from the lives of saints, encourages similar actions: inviting the poorest to the table and supporting them with food and drink. He also adds that "if high rank or public business hinders someone from this work, he will not lack a reward if he does it through others."[142]

It is important to remember that sometimes giving the poor your time and attention and showing them love are even more important than material support.

I can ask myself:
- What is my attitude towards the poor?
- How sensitive am I to their needs?
- To what extent do I show them respect and love?
- How much spiritual and material support do I offer them?

Act 4. **Ransoming captives.**

"*The ransoming of captives*, especially from infidels, O how glorious!"[143] Today, this act of mercy has changed into visiting prisoners. Saint Stanislaus cites examples of various saints who collected money or even offered themselves as slaves to ransom captives. He expressed surprise that in 17th century Poland so many of their compatriots remained in captivity under the Turks and Tatars.

Concluding his reflections on ransoming people from captivity, the Saint greatly broadens our horizons with the following conclusion: "Just consider how highly God values you, who value your own wealth as nothing, if you offer it to the poor."[144]

Today, we can translate this into visiting the imprisoned and supporting those in the greatest need. This work of mercy consists in giving a part of ourselves to others, something that is valuable to us and that we would not normally want to part with.

Act 5. **Covering the naked.**

We no longer encounter naked people on the streets, but the truly poor still live among us. Covering the nakedness of another person also means covering their material or spiritual poverty by defending them from judgment, ridicule, or rejection.

I can ask myself:

- What am I willing to offer to the poor I encounter every day?
- How much do I care about the fate of the poor in our country and around the world?
- To what extent do I see the suffering Christ in them?
- How willing am I to defend them from rejection or exclusion?

Act 6. Lodge Strangers.

"*To give lodging to strangers* is an act of great merit."[145] The following call from St. Stanislaus is very powerful and timely: "Woe to you, who perhaps feed many dogs and yet allow men to die of hunger! You, who close your doors to strangers, and keep even religious men away from your doors; will Christ not cast you out from the gate of Heaven? ... A guest comes, Christ comes. He who receives a guest, receives Christ."[146]

Some people today invest more energy and resources in saving animals than humans. Cruelty to animals or the killing of endangered species is treated as a crime and punished with imprisonment, which may be a good thing. However, simultaneously, abortion has become a "fundamental right of women" or a "human right" in many countries. Isn't this a paradox?

Of course, in a lighter form, this quotation refers to the disproportionate resources allocated to animals compared to that allocated for human use. Just ask those who have several cats how much they spend monthly on cat food. Do they spend at least as much on feeding or educating underprivileged children in their area or other countries?

"When a guest comes, Christ comes." How many homes and apartments today are completely closed to strangers, newcomers, or the poor! But at the same time, how many homes have opened their doors to our Ukrainian brothers and sisters forced to flee the Russian invaders since February 2022! Welcoming refugees into one's own home or supporting those who have done so is one of the contemporary manifestations of this act of mercy.

I can ask myself:

- How open am I to guests, both those who drop by for a moment and those who could stay for months or even years?
- How do I react to another ring of the doorbell or another phone call?
- How would people assess my hospitality and the openness of my home?
- To what extent do I see Christ's coming in every guest?
- What else can I do in this matter?

Act 7. Bury the dead.

"*To bury the dead free of charge,* simply out of charity, is not considered by God as a service of little value."[147] This act of mercy also includes providing selfless material and spiritual support to those grieving the death of a loved one.

Here we also receive very important words from St. Stanislaus (and not the only ones) about the necessity of praying for the deceased: "Certainly the most effective prayer is made by the one who, when he wishes to obtain God's mercy, shows mercy to a man. Yet what more eminent form of mercy can there be, than that shown to the dead, from whom no reward, no gratitude and no praise can be expected? Those who do this by all means gain immortal life for themselves."[148]

By praying for the deceased, we fulfill an act of mercy towards them, but at the same time, are transformed and open ourselves to receiving the mercy of the Lord for us. Receiving God's mercy and seeking it for others, including the deceased, leads us directly to eternal happiness.

You can ask yourself:

- How do I care for my deceased loved ones?
  What about the deceased in general?
- What more could I do for the deceased?

- To what extent do I support terminally ill individuals and their families? What can I offer them?
- What does my assistance to those who are in mourning look like?
- What else could I offer them?

SPIRITUAL ACTS OF MERCY

Undoubtedly, St. Stanislaus, the Prophet of the Immaculate Conception, dedicates more space in *The Mystical Temple of God* to acts of mercy for the soul than those of the body. Perhaps because he recognized that spiritual acts are not as obvious as corporal ones, he decided to provide us with more insights related to them. I have chosen only some of his thoughts here. Each of them can also be found in various spiritual guides, collections of wise sayings, etc. These points are not something you can absorb and accept all at once. Instead, they require calm reading and careful savoring of the content.

Act 1. **Giving advice.**

"*Giving advice*, sincere and salutary, to one who needs it, is the mark of a most virtuous mind. ... He who does this without a desire for a reward is truly merciful. For at some time or other, right advice is more useful than whatever great financial support. ... The gifts of the Holy Spirit should be spread out, ... and it is greed to want a reward for one's advice."[149]

Today, advisory firms are very popular in a variety of fields: law, construction, education, diet, and so on. If we are experts in a particular field, we can dedicate at least some of our time, knowledge, and skills to help the less fortunate for free. This is how volunteer-led advisory services are created, for example, in parish settings. Such service is one of the acts of mercy.

Act 2. **To forgive.**

"*To forgive* those who wrong us, and to be reconciled with our enemies, this — I say — is not just peculiarly Christian but distinctly divine. For in what manner do we more express the goodness of God than in forgiving offenses and loving our enemies?"[150]

Citing St. Paul's Letter to the Romans (Rom 5:6–8, 10), St. Stanislaus explains that Christ died for us when we were sinners and His enemies. He, the Creator and Savior, died for us, His enemies, so that we would not die for eternity. Therefore, forgiving our wrongdoers or enemies is only a reflection of the forgiveness we ourselves have received from God.

Saint Stanislaus is aware that such forgiveness is possible only through the power of God. That is precisely why he encourages us to forgive in this way. God grants us the power for such forgiveness, especially in the Eucharist.

Forgiveness does not consist in forgetting the wrongs done to us but in making a decision of the will. I not only do not want harm done to my wrongdoer, but I desire blessing for him or her. I wish this person well, and am willing to do good for him. I do not curse, I bless. To make this possible, we need our hearts transformed to resemble the Heart of Jesus. While hanging on the Cross, He repeated, "Father, forgive them; they do not know what they are doing." Although condemned and crucified for sins He did not commit, He loved His tormentors from the height of the Cross. When forgiving remains difficult for us, it is worth repeating this beautiful prayer: "Make our hearts like to Thine." Make my heart according to the Heart of Jesus, Father, so that I can forgive, love, and completely surrender myself to You.

Every day in the Lord's Prayer, we repeat, "Forgive us our trespasses, as we forgive those who trespass against us." My forgiveness pleases God. God forgives us in an absolute sense, but if we do not forgive others, our hearts are not open to receive His forgiveness of us. When we approach the Eucharist, we can ask God for the gifts of forgiveness, reconciliation, and love for those who have wronged us.

Saint Stanislaus concludes the reflections on forgiveness with a significant encouragement: "Listen to this, you, who nurture never-ending hatreds and foster continual rancor in your hearts, you are waiting for a chance for vengeance, and meanwhile, in the most Holy Eucharist, with Judas, you give kisses to Christ the Lord. If your trespasses are to be forgiven you, as you are used to forgive your enemies, then your salvation is lost, you have perished. Therefore 'love your enemies' as Jesus urges, 'that you may be children of your heavenly Father'" (*see* Mt 5:44–45).[151]

Perhaps today is indeed a good day to revisit past grievances and finally forgive my parents, friends, and superiors. It is worth at least asking God for the strength to forgive in this way. Nursing wounds is always detrimental to us and all of our relationships.

Act 3. Console the afflicted.

"*To console the afflicted,* not only by words but also by deeds, is a mercy not easily attained."[152] Saint Stanislaus encourages comforting the distressed with words, our presence and closeness, or even a gift. According to him, it is good to bring joy, even to a sorrowful enemy.

Comfort can be offered in various ways depending on the person's distress. If someone is lonely, elderly, or ill, you can visit and help with daily chores. You can bring a meal or do shopping, handle legal matters, or provide assistance in other ways. If someone is in mourning, you can express your closeness through a visit, phone call, or thoughtful gift. If a person has lost possessions or a job, you can offer material support, and so on. Many people tend to avoid someone in distress, not wanting to be intrusive or pushy. However, sometimes a small gesture, a smile, or a kind inquiry can bring comfort.

Comfort should be provided to a person in every kind of distress, but according to St. Stanislaus, the most painful problems are severe spiritual falls. For there is no greater unhappiness for a person than to become an enemy of God through sin. "Such men," he continues, "are to be helped and comforted in every way."[153] According to St. Stanislaus, appropriate support is well-applied by practicing the next work of mercy.

Act 4. **Admonishing sinners.**

Here, St. Stanislaus emphasizes that reprimands should be "prudent," meaning without "ardent zeal," and certainly never "with anger." Sometimes we tolerate many misdeeds of our children, fellow brothers, or colleagues, but upon reaching "the final straw," we explode with multiplied force.

Saint Stanislaus recommends admonishing others "in a gentle spirit," not revealing their errors until they have been admonished "fraternally in private," following the Gospel's guidance (Mt 18:15–17). He is aware that public revelation of our sins, mistakes, or flaws, sometimes only results in our readiness to defend them ardently. Therefore, admonitions must be wise, patient, and cautious. You must choose the right opportunity and the appropriate manner.

Saint Paul advises, "Brothers, even if one of you is caught doing something wrong, those of you who are spiritual should set that person right in a spirit of gentleness; and watch yourselves that you are not put to the test in the same way. Carry each other's burdens; that is how to keep the law of Christ" (Gal 6:1–2).

At the same time, we must remember, "Just as men gradually grow accustomed to their vices, equally they are to be withdrawn from them."[154] For this reason, there is no need to be pushy or forceful. There should also be no expectation of immediate results, even with the most appropriate admonition.

The most important part in this process is prayer, which can achieve what is humanly impossible, as St. Stanislaus explains: "[O]ne must most fervently pray to God for the obstinate and destitute of grace, that He may accomplish with His light what exceeds our prudence or authority ... . Here prayer helps more than harsh rebuke or severe blame."[155] When a person does not change his behavior and stubbornly clings to erroneous or even sinful actions especially after being admonished, St. Stanislaus advises that there is no point in arguing anymore. Instead, it is better to commend the person to God, because He can accomplish what is humanly impossible and even bring good out of evil.

For those who find it difficult to accept admonitions, St. Stanislaus reminds them of relevant passages from the Holy Scripture: "Better attend to the reprimand of the wise than listen to a song sung by a fool" (Eccl 7:5); "Trustworthy are blows from a friend, deceitful are kisses from a foe" (Prov 27:6).

Often, admonishing others seems so difficult and fruitless that we give up on it from the start. Saint Stanislaus says, "I do not permit connivance, since it destroys entire communities. In this regard I want charity to be joined to prudence and patience. ... [T]o fulfill the law of fraternal correction, it is sufficient to not approve an action, if corrections cannot be done otherwise."[156] Therefore, it is essential to make clear what I do not accept, and approve of, and what, in my opinion, requires change. For example, if words hostile to faith or the Church are constantly spoken in the workplace, I can at least decisively refrain from joining the chorus of critics. If people are constantly gossiping about absent individuals, I can point out their good qualities or at least remain silent. When indecent or vulgar stories and jokes are being told, instead of joining in the bursts of joy, I can express disapproval or leave the company.

At the end of this very long point, St. Stanislaus mentions prominent figures, starting from those in ancient times, who were willing to endure great suffering in opposition to evil, including death. He is aware, however, that not everyone is granted the grace of such martyrdom. He therefore recommends at least prayer and open disapproval, as mentioned earlier.

The section about admonishing others is likely so lengthy because St. Stanislaus first admonished the Piarists and then was himself admonished and punished by them until he left the order. He had vast experience in this area and, from his own experience, could advise on the ways that bring good results and those that, on the contrary, can lead to even greater obstinacy and hardness in sin.

Act 5. **Teaching the ignorant.**

Both as a Piarist and in the religious order he founded, St. Stanislaus devoted himself to teaching and catechizing the poor, including the poorest children. Teaching and instructing the common people, especially the poor, was considered the third mission of the Marian Fathers in the 18th and 19th centuries, alongside devotion to the Immaculate Conception of the Blessed Virgin Mary and prayer for the deceased. Saint Stanislaus emphasizes the importance of instructing the poor, not just any instruction but teaching them the truths necessary for salvation. Let us read an extended quotation:

> Those who will instill a knowledge, love, and fear of God in others' hearts, will come near to the titles of God's Mother. O how admirable are Christ's coworkers, who only in consideration of His love, sincerely and carefully put forth to children, especially to those who are ignorant and uncouth, or in error, all that is necessary for salvation, for leading life in a Christian way, for avoiding vices and embracing virtues. No work of mercy is more distinguished than this; none is more blessed.[157]

Saint Stanislaus recognizes that the work of teaching children "those things without which eternal salvation cannot be had"[158] is carried out by teachers, preachers, catechists, and parents. Therefore, on one hand, he thanks God for those who imparted the knowledge of God to him and led him to faith. On the other hand, he prays for pastors, preachers, and parish priests, asking God to bless them with light and zeal for teaching those entrusted to them.

Today, many parents strive to provide their children with education in every possible area. Young people participate in foreign language courses, music lessons, sports, and cultural activities, among others. However, sometimes parents neglect the religious education of their children and fail to nurture their faith. Unfortunately, sometimes the parents of a child preparing for First Communion are outraged that their child is required to attend Mass every Sunday. They may also protest when they see that their child is expected to participate in the Easter Triduum and various devotions before Confirmation. However, these are just the basics of faith, nothing extraordinary, the everyday life of Christians.

In the religious education and formation of children, grandparents can play a significant role. They often teach their grandchildren how to pray and bear witness to their faith and how God blesses them in their daily lives. The home of grandparents can be a crucial place to impart faith to their grandchildren.

It is worth thanking God for those who have passed on the Faith and knowledge of God to us. It is also worthwhile to pray for ourselves and all those in teaching, pastoral, and parenting roles so that we may fulfill the task entrusted to us of leading people to faith and to knowledge and love of God.

Act 6. **Praying for the souls in Purgatory.**

"Next, it is the greatest charity *to pray earnestly* to God for the freedom of the souls remaining in Purgatory, or to assist them by merciful alms as by various other means. Quite impious and foolish is he who is not moved by their torments, and does not help those who suffer when he can."[159]

The necessity of praying for the deceased was already mentioned in the context of burying the dead but is additionally justified and emphasized here. Intercession for the deceased includes not only prayer on their behalf but also almsgiving and "other means," left to our ingenuity.

Saint Stanislaus encourages interceding for the deceased for at least three reasons. Firstly, he refers to a story from the Old Testament about the battles of Judas Maccabeus. In one of the battles (*see* 2 Macc 12:38–46), a number of soldiers died. Hidden idols were found with each of them, which was forbidden. The other soldiers all understood that unfaithfulness to God was the reason for their death. The commander then ordered a collection of money taken and sent it to the temple in Jerusalem with a request for prayers for the fallen. The author of the book rightly appreciates this action and concludes that it was "an action altogether fine and noble, prompted by his belief in the Resurrection. For had he not expected the fallen to rise again, it would have been superfluous and foolish to pray for the dead" (2 Macc 12:43–44).

Secondly, in St. Stanislaus' time, the 17th century, the population of Poland decreased from about 11 million to six million. This was due to war, diseases, and famine. Armies passing through Poland, including Swedish, Tartar, Muscovite, Cossack, Hungarian, and others, brought death, diseases, and the destruction of homes, fields, orchards, livestock, and food supplies. Today's threats, like the COVID-19 epidemic, or even war itself, are incomparably smaller than those of the 17th century. Saint Stanislaus accompanied the sick and dying and was constantly faced with death. Hence, this explains his particular concern for the fate of souls who died suddenly and violently.

The third factor that influenced St. Stanislaus' choice of making prayer for the deceased a special mission of the Marian Fathers (the second goal of the order) were the visions of Purgatory that the Saint experienced multiple times. These visions were described, among others, by his biographer, Venerable Servant of God Casimir Wyszyński.[160] Here, I will mention just two of these events.

After Holy Mass in the Sanctuary of Our Lady in Studzianna, St. Stanislaus "became like a dead person and had a vision of being taken to Purgatory. There, witnessing the unbearable sufferings of souls, he heard the Blessed Virgin Mary and all the souls interceding with the Almighty God on his behalf, so that he would return to life to provide much-needed help to the deceased."[161] The Oratorians, who had charge of the shrine, seeing him during the vision, believed he had died. However, upon returning to life, "resembling a corpse, he appeared in the local church, which was crowded with people, ascended the pulpit, and delivered a magnificent, lengthy sermon on the urgent necessity of helping souls."[162] Upon returning to the community in the Marian Forest, "he established that the brothers of his congregation would forever pray the Office and the Rosary for the deceased every day, and that all merits, labors, fasts, mortifications, as well as other spiritual works and physical efforts, would be offered for the release of souls from unbearable suffering."[163]

While with King John III Sobieski in Ukraine, St. Stanislaus visited the graves of deceased soldiers and prayed for them. "One day, amidst these graves, many souls appeared to him, imploring him with trust and tears never to cease providing them with such help .... When he returned to his brethren, he instructed them to remember, in addition to others who had passed away, especially the souls of soldiers and those who died of the plague."[164]

As attested by his biographer, "among the brethren and strangers alike, it was already a widespread belief that every time he entered into ecstasy, he was always transported to purgatory."[165] For this reason, often, "with tears in his eyes, [he] fervently recommended the souls of the deceased"[166] to both the brethren and laypeople.

According to St. Stanislaus, an additional argument for interceding for the deceased is the fact that they also pray for us. "What about the fact that we shall have in Heaven as many Patrons and helpers as many souls we have brought there, thanks to our help, from the furnace of Purgatory!"[167]

"Support the deceased and encourage others to do so." Saint Stanislaus repeats this message even today.

Act 7. **Remit offenses.**

"The last work of Mercy, equal nonetheless to the others, is: *to remit offenses.*"[168]

Invoking St. Paul's admonition to forgive injuries (cf. 1 Cor 6:6–9), the Marian Founder calls, "I understand that he who suffers injuries is blessed; while the one who inflicts injury is unhappy. As much as the former will be exalted for disregarding vengeance, so much so the latter will be humbled by God for perpetrating injustice. It is good to forgive, but evil to irritate, offend, and oppress. In forgiving I imitate Christ; in oppressing me you emulate the torturers of Christ. Therefore I encourage that injuries be remitted, and discourage that they be inflicted."[169]

As St. Stanislaus mentioned in chapter 17 of *The Mystical Temple of God*, the roof of our temple is made up of our deeds; they bear witness to us and our lives. Each act of mercy renews the mystical temple (chapter 21), is directed towards God, and gains us His mercy. Whatever we have done to the least of these, we have done unto God, as St. Stanislaus reminds us. On the basis of acts of mercy, we will also hear, "Come, you whom my Father has blessed" (Mt 25:34–36).

Saint Stanislaus concludes the entire chapter on acts of mercy with words of encouragement and hope: "And so let us apply ourselves to the works of mercy, let us exert ourselves; through them we restore the Temples of God, our souls; we repair, I say, the inner man; we shall hear 'blessed,' and we shall possess the heavenly kingdom."[170]

It seems that among the 14 acts of mercy, supporting the dead was closest to St. Stanislaus, as it appears in the context of burying the deceased and occupies the entire reflection on supporting the living and the dead. He also assigned a significant role to teaching the truths of faith and bringing people closer to God, especially the poor, the uneducated, and children. The most extensive section is the one about admonishing sinners, where he examines various situations, both from the perspective of the one admonishing and the one being admonished.

It is valuable to reflect on each of these acts of mercy and conduct a personal examination of conscience.

To what extent are these acts of mercy a permanent part of my life?

What more could I do?

How could I do them better?

"Let the body be subject to the spirit, and the spirit to reason and the law; let us become conformed to the image of the Son of God, and we shall become coheirs of His heavenly kingdom: if we suffer with Him, we shall be glorified with Him."

St. Stanislaus Papczyński

CHAPTER 10

Eternity[171]

The mystical temple which we are was consecrated and dedicated by God at the moment of our Baptism. It is not intended solely for earthly life but anticipates its fulfillment in the glory of Heaven. Our patron saints are a ray of hope and a promise of Heaven, serving as guardians of the temple.

PATRON SAINTS AS GUARDIANS

"Our singular Guardians, who are to be revered by us with singular honor are: the most August and Supereminent Virgin, the Mother of God, our guardian angel, and the saint whose name, as given us, we have."[172]

Mary. There are two dangerous extremes in the approach to Mary today. Some believe that "you can never have enough of Mary" and sometimes devote more time, energy, and devotion to her than to God Himself. They may even attribute almost divine attributes to her and, at times, contrast her love with the "severity of God." On the other hand, there are those who believe that all prayers should be addressed directly to God and disapprove of any Marian devotion. Saint Stanislaus Papczyński is remarkably balanced and clear on this issue.

He believed that "we have all things through Mary" and that, after God, she is the most important. In his teachings, the Prophet of the Immaculate Conception explains that only God deserves adoration. Mary, however, is venerated as the first among the saints, in a special and sublime way, but not comparable to the worship of God Himself. As she cared for her Son during His earthly life, she cares for us today. Keeping in mind the story of the wedding at Cana in Galilee, we can be sure that Mary presents our needs to her Son before we even recognize or realize them ourselves.

In the teachings of St. Stanislaus, there is an interesting distinction between following (*sequela*) only Christ and imitating (*imitatio*) Jesus, Mary, and other saints. He explains that all the graces that Mary possesses and distributes come ultimately from the salvific work of Jesus Christ. There is no doubt here that there is one Triune God, and Mary is the most important of His creations as the Mother of the Son of God and our Mother, perfectly cooperating with God and always filled with His grace.

The Guardian Angel. "Our second guardian is the Angel, to whose guardianship we were entrusted soon after we began to exist."[173] Saint Stanislaus assures us that our guardian angels love us. This is the reason "they do not neglect even the greatest sinner, yet to his last breath continually watching for his conversion."[174] Therefore, he recommends praying to our Guardian Angel and listening to "this Holy Spirit, given ... by God the father of the heavenly luminaries as [our] guide and leader."[175]

It is interesting to note that when St. Stanislaus returned from Rome, he brought with him only two paintings: one of St. Michael the Archangel and the other of St. Raphael the Archangel, as he held both in great reverence.

The biographer of St. Stanislaus, Venerable Servant of God Casimir Wyszyński, mentions that, when passing by a village or town, he would pay homage to the guardian angels of the residents of those places by reciting nine Hail Mary's.

In today's literature and film, angels often appear as spiritual beings, but they may not necessarily have any connection to God and instead reflect the fantasies and desires of their creators. However, angels are spiritual creatures created by God and sent by Him for our salvation. Each person has a guardian angel, but there are also archangels sent by God for special tasks. To demonstrate this, it is sufficient to mention the Archangel Gabriel, sent with the message first to Zechariah and then to Mary; the Archangel Raphael, who accompanied Tobias on his journey; and the Archangel Michael, the leader of the heavenly armies. Invoking their protection, care, and guidance always brings good results.

Saint Stanislaus assures us that the **patron saints of our Baptism and Confirmation** also continually recommend us to God: "They favor our good deeds, favor our merits, favor our happiness, and await us with far greater longing than companions in port await the shipwrecked."[176]

He suggests celebrating the feasts of our patrons with an octave and honoring them each day during the octave with pious and good deeds, such as prayer, penance, almsgiving, forgiveness, acts of mercy, etc. "Finally we should perform whatever is acceptable to God, whatever brings honor to our patrons and whatever is salutary to us and our neighbor, because of our love and reverence due to them. In this way we shall have honored our Guardians in the best way."[177] It turns out that even honoring the saints should be done in a way that pleases God and contributes to His greater glory. In the life of the Marian Founder, the Holy Trinity was always first and foremost.

It is worth mentioning that in the *Rule of Life*, the Marian Fathers are prescribed a special fast on "the Vigils of the seven Feasts of Our Lady, and of Saints Michael the Archangel, Joseph, Stanislaus and Anna, with one meal or by limiting yourselves to bread and water."[178]

Venerable Casimir writes about the great devotion with which St. Stanislaus venerated the Immaculate Conception and Mary Immaculate. The patrons of the Congregation during St. Stanislaus' time that Venerable Casimir mentions includes St. Michael the Archangel, St. Joseph, Sts. Peter and Paul, St. Stanislaus the Bishop, and St. Stanislaus Kostka. Venerable Casimir claims that St. Stanislaus also honored "many other patrons" in various ways.

Today, alongside the main Patroness, Mary Immaculate, St. Stanislaus, and Venerable Casimir, the Marian Fathers also list the following patrons: Blessed George Matulewicz, Blessed George Kaszyra, Blessed Anthony Leszczewicz, St. Michael the Archangel, St. Joseph, Sts. Peter and Paul, St. Francis of Assisi, St. Thomas Aquinas, St. Joan of France, St. Ignatius of Loyola, St. Vincent de Paul, St. Faustina, and Pope St. John Paul II.

Just as excessive or inappropriate veneration of the saints can lead us away from God, neglecting the veneration of the saints and our heavenly patrons can lead us straight to Protestantism and a rationalization of faith. Relating to the saints and our patrons is intended to connect us with the residents of Heaven, shed light on our lives, and provide support from those who have already attained eternal happiness.

It is worthwhile to choose additional, personal patrons for our mystical temple. Sometimes, at different stages of life, we have a special relationship with various saints. Some accompany us throughout our lives. In recent times, St. Stanislaus has become a special patron for many people, often referred to as a "powerhouse of God," the Prophet of the Immaculate Conception, and the patron of unborn life.

Points for personal prayer:

- Which patron saints do I particularly reverence?
- How do I celebrate the feast days of my patrons?
- When and how do I ask for their intercession?
- What more can I do in the veneration of my patron saints?

IMMORTALITY OF THE TEMPLE

Saint Stanislaus references various passages from the Holy Scripture and the statements of the saints to assure that the entire temple is immortal: both the soul and the body. "Nothing is more consistent with reason than this perpetuity of our Mystical Temple."[179]

He teaches that our bodies will decompose in the earth and be assimilated by other living creatures (worms, birds, etc.) but, at the end of time, will be resurrected in a new form. This is testified by the Holy Scripture, the changing seasons, caterpillars and butterflies, and the entire nature that surrounds us. He rhetorically asks, if God leads nature from its winter dormancy to the springtime bloom, would He not awaken the bodies laid in the grave to new life?

In contrast to the body, the soul is not subject to decay. It is inherently immortal because "this [breath], however, which the Divine mouth (if I may use a human way of speaking) has breathed onto the face of man, is immortal as God Himself from whom it began."[180]

For St. Stanislaus, the immortality of souls is natural and self-evident. "[A]s soon as they have departed from the body they fly out either to glory or punishment, which is either temporary or everlasting."[181] Of course, the outcome of the final judgment depends on our life. "For those who imitated Christ in life, will attain the glory of Christ; but those who confessed Him with their lips, yet denied Him in their heart, who preached Him by words and blasphemed Him by their deeds, will descend alive into hell."[182]

In *The Mystical Temple of God*, St. Stanislaus does not present the possibility of hell just to frighten or create confusion. Rather, he desires our conversion and purification. He places us in the perspective of eternity so that we may live our earthly lives more fully, because when we lose sight of the ultimate goal, our earthly existence can become an unbearable drama or a cycle of sin without hope. Living on Earth "as if God did not exist" can lead to a situation where we will not see Him even after death. And that, precisely, will be the greatest suffering of hell. God is love for all eternity, but through our sinful actions and choices, we can separate ourselves from Him forever, the source of our life and joy.[183]

Holy St. Stanislaus provides two conclusions to chapter 23 of *The Mystical Temple of God*. One is from St. Paul's letter: "Since these promises have been made to us, my dear friends, we should wash ourselves clean of everything that pollutes either body or spirit, bringing our sanctification to completion in the fear of God" (2 Cor 7:1). The second one, concluding the chapter, is purely from himself: "Let the body be subject to the spirit, and the spirit to reason and the law; let us become conformed to the image of the Son of God, and we shall become coheirs of His heavenly kingdom: if we suffer with Him, we shall be glorified with Him."[184]

Points for personal prayer:

- To what extent can I say today that I resemble the image of the Son of God?
- To what extent does the perspective of eternity influence and shape my choices and actions in this earthly life?
- How much do I desire Heaven, and what actions do I take to make it my inheritance?
- Ask God to remove the fear of death and bestow upon you the graces of desiring Heaven and living today in complete unity with the Holy Trinity.

THE GLORY OF THE TEMPLE

Many people would like to know what Heaven will be like, how we will look and behave, and what kind of bodies we will have. Saint Stanislaus tries to answer some of these questions, referring, as usual, to the Holy Scriptures and the sayings of the saints.

Our heavenly bodies, he says, will be characterized by four qualities: impassibility, subtlety, agility, and clarity. All these attributes can be seen in Christ after His Resurrection, and we will be endowed with these qualities as well. Impassibility of the body means the absence of any pain, discomfort, or corruption of the body for all eternity, because, after rising from the dead, Christ no longer suffers and dies. Subtlety is the ability to penetrate all matter like the Risen One, Who left the tomb without breaking it and entered the disciples' midst despite closed doors.

Agility or swiftness is the ability to move quickly (or instantaneously) in any direction, just as the Risen One appeared to the disciples in different places at close to the same time. The clarity of bodies invokes a passage from the book of Daniel: "Of those who are sleeping in the Land of Dust, many will awaken, some to everlasting life, some to shame and everlasting disgrace. Those who are wise will shine as brightly as the expanse of the heavens, and those who have instructed many in uprightness, as bright as stars for all eternity" (Dan 12:2–3). We can also refer to the transformed and radiant face of the Lord on the Mount of Transfiguration and after the Resurrection. We await, as St. Stanislaus explains through St. Paul, the transformation of our bodies to be like the glorious body of Jesus Christ.[185]

Saint Stanislaus also mentions that all the senses (sight, hearing, taste, touch, and smell) will be satisfied in a new way and will be a source of spiritual delight.

In his work *Examination of the Heart*, St. Stanislaus similarly speaks about Heaven, the attributes of the glorified body (instead of subtlety, he mentions immortality), the delights of the senses, and the happiness of both soul and body. He explains that the greatest happiness is the contemplation of God (just as the greatest unhappiness for souls in hell is the inability to be with God for eternity). In the last point of *Examination of the Heart*, in his reflection on the last things for Sunday evening, St. Stanislaus encourages:

> Consider that the vision of God alone excels all the goods that the blessed possess in Heaven. This vision is the source out of which all the glory flows; all the abundance of beatitude comes forth; all the happiness descends upon all the heavenly beings, so that the heavenly inheritance itself, which the Savior of the world promised to His followers, depends upon this very beatific vision. ... So you see, of what great goods miserable sinners despoil themselves; indeed, of what great goods you despoil yourself whenever you do not want to strive lawfully![186]

In *The Mystical Temple of God*, St. Stanislaus describes the ultimate reality of Heaven with extraordinary delicacy and sensitivity, as if he does not want to exaggerate anything. He also emphasizes multiple times that it is better to strive to attain Heaven than to try to understand it today, because what we will experience will far exceed all our expectations and desires. "May God make us understand these things rather than describe them. May the most blessed Trinity have us reach the end for which we were created, redeemed, and called to by faith."[187]

"May it safeguard us in this most perilous and stormy ocean of our present lives so that we do not suffer the shipwreck of our eternal lives, but reach the port of the most longed for blessedness with Christ as captain, Mary as guiding star, the Angels as oarsmen, and the saints' intercession as the winds."[188] Here, again the beautiful depiction of the spiritual reality and our "guardians" is, as always, very vivid and evocative.

Saint Stanislaus "closes and seals" the mystical temple with the "Admonition" drawn from the writings of St. Bernard. This is a beautiful summary of the entire *Mystical Temple of God* and a clear guide for those who want to progress on the path of spiritual life and become an increasingly beautiful mystical temple of God Himself: "Therefore, use yourself as a Temple of God, because of that within you which is like to God. Since the supreme honor shown to God is to worship and imitate Him. You imitate Him if you are devout, you worship Him if you are merciful. Do everything like the Son of God, that you may be worthy of Him who deigned to call you son."[189]

At the end of the text, St. Stanislaus includes the "Inscription of the Mystical Temple," a kind of dedication (*dedicatio*). It is a response to the consecration (*consecratio*) that God performed in us in Baptism and to the re-consecration (*reconsecratio*) that He accomplishes in us every time we receive the Sacraments of Reconciliation and the Eucharist.

Saint Stanislaus dedicates himself, i.e. the temple described above, to the Eternal Father, his Creator; to the Eternal Son, his Redeemer; and to the Eternal Spirit, his Sanctifier. He dedicates himself in response to the consecration performed by God and in anticipation of the consecration that God will accomplish in him, "now and forever."

It is worth repeating the last "Admonition" within ourselves. It is also worth repeating my dedication to God in the Holy Trinity. He is the Lord of eternity. He can lift me from sins. He can keep me from sins. Only He can sanctify me for eternity.

Conclusion

The book *The Mystical Temple of God* begins by assuring us that we are created in the image and likeness of God and, through Baptism, consecrated as His mystical temple. The final chapters speak of immortality and the glory to which this temple, all of us, are invited and destined. God the Father, Jesus Christ, the Holy Spirit, all the gifts and actions of the Lord God, the saints — everything — serves to assist us in reaching the goal for which we were created and consecrated: eternal happiness with God in Heaven. All that is needed in this life is our commitment and dedication to God in building and adorning His temple.

> May we be holy and unblemished before His presence now and forever!
> May we, as His mystical temples, radiate His splendor, His holiness, and His glory now and forever!
> This is God's plan and promise and our task and desire.
> Let it be fulfilled!
> Amen.

Bibliography

Papczyński, St. Stanislaus. *Selected Writings.* Warsaw: PROMIC; Stockbridge, Massachusetts: Marian Heritage, 2022.

Wyszyński, Casimir, MIC. *Opowieść o Świętym Stanisławie Papczyńskim napisana w XVIII wieku uzupełniona w XXI wieku* [The Story of Saint Stanislaus Papczyński, written in the 18th century, supplemented in the 21st century]. https://stanislawpapczynski.org/his-life.

About the Author

Born in 1966, Fr. Paweł Naumowicz, MIC, joined the Congregation of Marian Fathers after completing his studies at the Gdańsk University of Technology. After his ordination in 1997, he served as a director of vocations, prefect of seminarians, and provincial superior in Poland.

Father Naumowicz obtained his doctorate in sacred theology from the Pontifical Gregorian University in Rome, focusing on the spirituality of St. Stanislaus Papczyński in the light of the Immaculate Conception.

Since 2020, he has been rector at the Shrine of St. Stanislaus in Marianki, Góra Kalwaria, Poland.

Endnotes

[1] See St. Stanislaus Papczyński, *The Mystical Temple of God* (*Templum Dei Mysticum*), in Papczyński, *Selected Writings*, 565–673 (PROMIC and Marian Heritage, 2022, Warsaw, Stockbridge, MA). Hereafter abbreviated as *TDM*.

[2] See St. Stanislaus Papczyński, *Self-Offering* (*Oblatio*), in *Selected Writings*, 864–873. Hereafter abbreviated as *Oblatio*.

[3] See St. Stanislaus Papczyński, *Rule of Life* (*Norma Vitae*), in *Selected Writings*, 49–79. Hereafter abbreviated as *NV*.

[4] See *TDM*, 569–673.

[5] Biblical passages quoted from *The New Jerusalem Bible* (NJB), Darton, Longman, and Todd and *Les Éditions du Cerf*, 1985. However, some passages are adapted to the translations of the *Vulgate*, from which St. Stanislaus read directly.

[6] See *NV*, 49–79.

[7] See *Oblatio*, 864–873.

[8] *NV*, 66.

[9] *TDM*, 571–572.

[10] It's worth paying attention to the word *trutino* often used by St. Stanislaus, which means "I chew" or "I ruminate." It is a *technical* expression of the Desert Fathers. The way ruminants eat served as an allegorical illustration of a contemplative hermit, who was to repeat a given or chosen biblical text in a low voice throughout the day, savoring it and, through contemplation, perfectly assimilating it.

[11] See *TDM*, chapters 1–2.

[12] *TDM*, 574.

[13] Ibid., 574, 576.

[14] Ibid., 579-580.

[15] Ibid., 575.

[16] See St. Stanislaus Papczyński, *Examination of the Heart (Inspectio Cordis)*, in *Selected Writings*, 111–563. Hereafter abbreviated as *IC*. *Inspectio Cordis* is a collection of points for meditation on Sundays and feast days, as well as special reflections for retreat days and each day of the week. Saint Stanislaus Papczyński preached them to the Piarists in Góra Kalwaria. Father Thaddaeus Lancton, MIC, writes a weekly series based on *Inspectio Cordis* that is posted on www.Marian.org.

[17] See St. Stanislaus Papczyński, *The First Testament*, 926–929; *Second Testament*, 933–940; *Profession of Solemn Vows*, 941–943, all in *Selected Writings*.

[18] *TDM*, 577.

[19] Ibid., 580.

[20] Ibid., 580.

[21] See St. Stanislaus Papczyński, *Messenger of the Queen of Arts*, in *Selected Writings*, 81–106. This rhetoric textbook written by St. Stanislaus was first published in 1663 (with subsequent editions in 1664, 1665, and 1669). It was widely used in Piarist colleges for over 100 years.

[22] *TDM*, chap. 19.

[23] One can also contemplate the conversion story of a servant of the Ethiopian queen and his Baptism by Philip (Acts 8:26–40). There, too, catechesis, a confession of faith, and Baptism were sufficient to admit a Gentile into the community of the Church and the ranks of the saved.

[24] *TDM*, 635.

[25] For example, in the Second Vatican Council document *Lumen Gentium*, n. 44, *consecratio* is reserved for expressing the actions of God. Human acts of dedication are described using verbs like *dedicare* and *devovere*.

[26] "The other is the one by which, observing the annual memory of that first Consecration [*dedicatio*] we give God true thanks for our sanctification [*consecratio*] and celebrate our most joyous feast of consecration in a spirit of gratitude by renewing our fervor to serve God." *TDM*, 635.

[27] Ibid., 635.

[28] Ibid., 636

[29] Ibid., 636.

[30] Ibid.

[31] Ibid., 637.

[32] Ibid., 638.

[33] See Ibid., chaps. 3–6.

[34] Ibid., 581.

[35] Ibid., 582.

[36] Ibid.

[37] Ibid., 583.

[38] Ibid., 583–584.

[39] Ibid., 584.

[40] Ibid., 590.

[41] Ibid., 591.
[42] *NV*, 60.
[43] See Ibid., 59–60.
[44] Ibid., 60.
[48] See St. Stanislaus Papczyński, *The Crucified Orator (Orator Crucifixis)*, in *Selected Writings*, 679–747.
[49] See St. Stanislaus Papczyński, *The Suffering Christ (Christus Patiens)*, in *Selected Writings*, 749–814.
[50] *TDM*, 588.
[51] Ibid., 589.
[52] Ibid.
[53] Ibid., 592.
[54] Ibid., 595.
[55] Ibid., 596.
[45] *TDM*, 585.
[46] Ibid., 586.
[47] *Oblatio*, 871–872.

[56] Ibid.
[57] Ibid.
[58] Ibid., 596–597
[59] Ibid., 597–598.
[60] See Ibid., chapters 7–8, 10.

[61] Saint Stanislaus writes about the Lord's prayer in Gethsemane in the first of seven meditations found in his book *The Suffering Christ* and in the reflection on the Lord's Passion intended for Monday morning, contained in *Examination of the Heart*. See *CP*, 749–814; *IC*, 537–538.

[62] *TDM*, 599.
[63] Ibid., 600.
[64] Ibid.
[65] Ibid., 601.
[66] Ibid.
[67] Ibid., 602.
[68] Ibid.
[69] Ibid., 603–604.
[70] Ibid., 608.
[71] Ibid.
[72] Ibid., 609.
[73] Ibid.
[74] Ibid., 610.
[75] Ibid.
[76] Ibid.
[77] *IC*, 230, 232.
[78] Ibid., 211–212.

[79] *TDM*, 611.
[80] See Ibid., chaps 13–15.
[81] Ibid., 617.
[82] Ibid., 621.
[83] Ibid., 620.
[84] Ibid., 621.
[85] Ibid.
[86] Ibid., 623.
[87] Ibid., 622–623.
[88] Ibid., 623.
[89] Ibid.
[90] Ibid., 623–624.
[91] Ibid., 618.
[92] Ibid.
[93] Ibid.
[94] *NV*, 64–65.

[95] Saint Stanislaus Papczyński, *Ordinances for the Korabiew Hermitage*, in *Selected Writings*, 945. The document was most likely created in June 1701, at the conclusion of the visitation of the first Marian religious house.

[96] *TDM*, 619.
[97] Ibid., 619–620.
[98] Ibid., 624.
[99] See Ibid., chaps 9, 11–12, 17–18.
[100] Ibid., 611.
[101] Ibid., 613.
[102] Ibid., 614.
[103] Ibid., 615.
[104] Ibid.
[105] Ibid.
[106] Ibid., 617.
[107] Ibid., 628.
[108] Ibid., 630.
[109] Ibid.
[110] Ibid.
[111] Ibid., 631.
[112] Ibid., 632
[113] Ibid., 634.
[114] Ibid., 632.

[115] Ibid., 604. The virtues particularly needed by the Marians are described by St. Stanislaus Papczyński in the reflections intended for retreats and found in *Examination of the Heart*. Among them are obedience, chastity, poverty, love, humility, temperance, prudence, kindness, graciousness, and gentleness. He also advises that each Marian frequently examine his conscience, observing his virtues and faults, in order to develop the former and eliminate the latter. See *IC*, 491–524.

[116] *TDM*, 605.
[117] Ibid., 607.
[118] See Ibid., chaps 16 and 22.
[119] Ibid., 657.
[120] Ibid., 625.
[121] Ibid.
[122] Ibid.
[123] Ibid.

[124] Ibid., 926.
[125] Ibid., 627.
[126] Ibid., 628.
[127] Ibid., 656–657.
[128] Ibid., 657.
[129] Ibid.
[130] Ibid.
[131] Ibid., 658.
[132] Ibid.
[133] Ibid.
[134] Ibid., 659.
[135] Ibid., 659–660.
[136] Ibid., 660–661.
[137] See Ibid., chap. 21.
[138] Ibid., 640–641.
[139] Ibid., 641
[140] Ibid.
[141] Ibid., 641 (italics in the original).
[142] Ibid., 642.
[143] Ibid. (italics in the original).
[144] Ibid., 644.
[145] Ibid., 645 (italics in original).
[146] Ibid.
[147] Ibid. (italics in original).
[148] Ibid.
[149] Ibid., 646 (italics in original).
[150] Ibid., (italics in original).
[151] Ibid., 647.
[152] Ibid., 648 (italics in original).
[153] Ibid., 649.
[154] Ibid.
[155] Ibid., 650.
[156] Ibid., 651.
[157] Ibid., 653.
[158] Ibid.
[159] Ibid., 654 (italics in original).
[160] See C. Wyszyński, *Opowieść o Świętym Stanisławie Papczyńskim napisana w XVIII wieku uzupełniona w XXI wieku* [*The Story of Saint Stanislaus Papczyński*, written in the 18th century, supplemented in the 21st century], p. 65–73. https://stanislawpapczynski.org/his-life). Hereafter abbreviated as *Vita*.
[161] *Vita*, 66.
[162] Ibid.
[163] *Vita*, 66–67.
[164] Ibid., 69.
[165] Ibid., 70.
[166] Ibid., 70–71.
[167] *TDM*, 655.
[168] Ibid. (italics in original).
[169] Ibid.
[170] Ibid., 656.
[171] See Ibid., chapters 20, 23–24.
[172] Ibid., 638.
[173] Ibid., 639.
[174] Ibid.
[175] Ibid.
[176] Ibid., 640.
[177] Ibid.
[178] *NV*, 65.
[179] *TDM*, 663.
[180] Ibid., 664.
[181] Ibid., 665.
[182] Ibid., 665-666.
[183] Saint Stanislaus writes more about the punishments and sufferings of hell in his reflections on the last things for Friday and Saturday evenings. See *IC*, 555–556, 558–560.
[184] *TDM*, 666.
[185] "But our homeland is in heaven and it is from there that we are expecting a Savior, the Lord Jesus Christ, who will transfigure the wretched body of ours into the mold of his glorious body, through the working of the power which he has, even to bring all things under his mastery" (Phil 3:20–21).
[186] *IC*, 562–563.
[187] *TDM*, 669-670.
[188] Ibid., 670.
[189] Ibid., 671.

Join the

Association of Marian Helpers,

headquartered at the National Shrine of The Divine Mercy, and share in special blessings!

An invitation from
Fr. Joseph, MIC, director

Marian Helpers is an Association of Christian faithful of the Congregation of Marian Fathers of the Immaculate Conception.

By becoming a member, you share in the spiritual benefits of the daily Masses, prayers, and good works of the Marian priests and brothers.

This is a special offer of grace given to you by the Church through the Marian Fathers. Please consider this opportunity to share in these blessings, along with others whom you would wish to join into this spiritual communion.

1-800-462-7426 • Marian.org/join

Spiritual Enrollments & Masses

Enroll your loved ones in the Association of Marian Helpers, and they will participate in the graces from the daily Masses, prayers, good works, and merits of the Marian priests and brothers around the world.

Request a Mass to be offered by the Marian Fathers for your loved ones

    Individual Masses
    (for the living or deceased)

    Gregorian Masses
    (30 days of consecutive Masses for the deceased)

1-800-462-7426 • Marian.org/enrollments • Marian.org/mass